TRANSLATION AND IMPLEMENTATION OF EVIDENCE-BASED PRACTICE

Building Social Work Research Capacity

Series Editor
Joan Levy Zlotnik, PhD

Doctoral Education
Jeane W. Anastas

Building Research Culture and Infrastructure
Ruth G. McRoy, Jerry P. Flanzer, and Joan Zlotnik

Research Integrity and Responsible Conduct of Research
Ann Nichols-Casebolt

Translation and Implementation of Evidence-Based Practice
Lawrence A. Palinkas and Haluk Soydan

Translation and Implementation of Evidence-Based Practice

Lawrence A. Palinkas
Haluk Soydan

OXFORD
UNIVERSITY PRESS

Published in the United States of America by Oxford University Press, Inc.,
198 Madison Avenue, New York, NY, 10016
United States of America

Oxford University Press, Inc., publishes works that further Oxford University's
objective of excellence in research, scholarship, and education

Oxford is a registered trade mark of Oxford University Press
in the UK and in certain other countries

Library of Congress Cataloging-in-Publication Data

Palinkas, Lawrence A.
   Translation and implementation of evidence-based practice / Lawrence A. Palinkas,
Haluk Soydan.
      p. cm. — (Building social work research capacity)
   Includes bibliographical references and index.
   ISBN 978-0-19-539848-9 (pbk.: alk. paper) 1. Evidence-based social work.
2. Social service—Practice. 3. Social service—Research. I. Soydan, Haluk, 1946– II. Title.
   HV10.5.P35 2012
   361.3'2—dc23   2011030842

Typeset in Chaparral Pro Regular
Printed on acid-free paper
Printed in United States of America

To our spouses, Terri and Leticia, for all your years of devotion to us and to the human services.

Contents

Preface

This book is about conducting research on the process and outcomes of the translation and implementation of evidence-based practices in social work. Its aim is to outline a strategy for conducting such research and identify the infrastructure and resources necessary to support such research within the field of social work. Using the National Institutes of Health (NIH) Roadmap as a guide, the book describes the challenges of investigating the process and outcomes of efforts to translate and implement evidence-based social work practice. It also describes a community-based participatory approach and use of mixed-methods designs to address these challenges. It begins at the point where research evidence gained from observational and experimental studies is translated into real-world settings of social work practice. Using the nomenclature found in the NIH Roadmap, this typically occurs in the context of effectiveness studies. The book then proceeds to discuss research on processes of dissemination and implementation of practices found to be both efficacious and effective. It is unique in that it provides case studies of research on the translation and implementation in social work practice, identifies potential barriers to conducting such research, and offers recommendations and guidelines for addressing these barriers. With the ongoing debate within the field of social work as to the value of evidence-based practice, as well as the recent efforts by NIH, Centers for Disease Control and Prevention, other government agencies, and private foundations to solicit applications for research on translation and implementation of evidence-based practice, it would seem that the time is ripe for a book that can help to develop the infrastructure necessary for conducting such research by and for social workers.

A major challenge for social work research is the application of sound research principles and practices that will address the barriers to dissemination and implementation of evidence-based practice. Equally important is that such research be relevant and usable to the social and health services practitioners and consumers. Translational research aims to develop effective methods of facilitating diffusion of innovations and to ensure the use of research results in social work practice (and other professions). Narrowing the gap between research and utilization is of tremendous significance to social work research as well as to social work practice and clients.

We wish to acknowledge the support we received through funding from the National Institute of Mental Health (P30 MH074678–03, John Landsverk, P.I.; P30 MH082760–03, Kenneth Wells, P.I.) and the William T. Grant Foundation (No. 10648, Lawrence Palinkas, P.I.). We also wish to acknowledge our colleagues engaged in translational research, whose invaluable advice and support helped to shape the ideas contained in this book. Among others, this distinguished group of scholars includes the following: Greg Aarons, John Brekke, Hendricks Brown, Patti Chamberlain, Bruce Chorpita, Kathy Ell, Ann Garland, Charles Glisson, Sally Horwitz, John Landsverk, Enola Proctor, Sonja Schoenwald, John Weisz, and Ken Wells. We are also thankful to Joan Levy Zlotnik, Oxford University Press series editor, and anonymous reviewers for valuable comments and guidance. Finally, we wish to acknowledge the tireless efforts of Eric Lindberg of the Hamovitch Center for Science in the Human Services. His editing skills proved to be critical in helping us "translate" our thoughts into words.

TRANSLATION AND IMPLEMENTATION OF EVIDENCE-BASED PRACTICE

1

Introduction

This book is conceived in response to the needs of social work professionals and members of other human services for effective and timely *utilization* of the *best available scientific evidence* on what works and what is potentially harmful. During the past 20 years, much progress has taken place in terms of our ability to develop and use increasingly sophisticated means of searching, retrieving, assessing, synthesizing, and disseminating rigorous evidence on effective interventions in social work practice and other human services; yet researchers, decision makers, and professionals remain concerned that too few evidence-based interventions are effectively used in service delivery and too many services currently in use lack an evidence base informed by scientific research.

The journey from "bench to trench," that is, from research to practice, is long, and that has continued to be a major concern of the profession. This journey includes knowledge production through basic, applied and other types of research; dissemination, receipt, acceptance, and use of research results by professional practitioners; translation of research results in accordance with local and client circumstances and the implementation of results in real-life treatment situations.

In the United States, several reports have highlighted the gap between evidence production and evidence utilization. In the field of health and mental health, three important reports have warned that the interval between production and utilization might be as long as 20 years (U.S. Department of Health and Human Services, 1999; Institute of Medicine, 2001; President's New Freedom Commission on Mental Health, 2003). In one remarkable study, McGlynn and colleagues (2003) demonstrated the deficit pertaining to preventive, acute, and long-term health care provided to Americans. The results were disappointing. Using 439 indicators of quality of care applied to 30 chronic and acute conditions, as well as preventive care, they documented the extent to which patients are deprived of recommended care. For example, approximately 25% of patients with breast cancer were not treated in accordance with recommended guidelines. Another relatively "better off" condition was coronary artery disease; however, only 68% of these patients received recommended care. In other words, nearly a third of the patients with coronary artery disease did not receive recommended care. At the other end of the scale, only 36.7% of patients with sexually transmitted diseases were treated with recommended guidelines. Alcohol dependency ranked lowest; amazingly, 90% of these patients were not treated with recommended care processes. Altogether, Americans in this study received only 50% of the recommended preventive, acute, and long-term health care. McGlynn and colleagues (2003, p. 2644) concluded that the identified deficits "pose serious threats to the health and well-being of the U.S. public."

In the realm of social work and mental health, Brekke, Ell, and Palinkas (2007) summarized some of the pertinent issues related to the gap between research and practice. For example, in the case of mental health services for clients with severe mental disorders, there is a "serious gap between what is known about mental disorders and their treatment from university-based clinical research and the services that are actually provided to consumers in typical community practice settings" (p. 124), and when evidence-based interventions are implemented in community settings, the fidelity to model prescriptions is inconsistent. There is strong evidence that guideline-based interventions are not widely implemented in general health care settings (p. 125). Sadly, mental health services for children and adolescents seem to be in worse shape than physical health services. Amassed evidence shows that mental health services for children and adolescents commonly implement value-driven interventions that lack evidence of effectiveness, and the implementation of interventions supported by evidence of efficacy and effectiveness remains an exception in community care settings. It is regrettable for the profession that this deficit is very common despite the fact that many psychotherapeutic and pharmacologic treatments have repeatedly been proved to be beneficial (p. 125).

From this perspective, the translation of evidence-based research results is necessary, and the implementation of useable knowledge and tools has become the focus of substantial new research initiatives and activities. Thus, the mission of this book is to provide an understanding of the state of the art of translational and implementation research in social work, how such research can support the profession through the betterment of client services, and how it may be best performed to accomplish the task of bringing the best available evidence to the service of professionals and their clients.

We acknowledge that translation and implementation of research do not necessarily pertain to evidence-based practices alone. Some may argue that research on social work practices other than those that are evidence based also requires translation and implementation to be deliverable to clients and patients. We do not disagree with this contention. However, it is our position that clients and patients in social work and other human services deserve the most effective, safest, and most affordable interventions and should not under any circumstances be exposed to interventions that might cause harm. From this ethical and professional standpoint, we dedicate this book to the translation and implementation of evidence-based practices. Our language excludes any social work interventions that are proved to be *harmful* (e.g., Scared Straight programs for delinquent adolescents) (Petrosino et al., 2004) or *lack evidence* because their potential harmfulness is not known (e.g., Michigan Family Reunification Program for emotional abuse, physical neglect and abuse, and sexual abuse) (California Evidence-Based Clearinghouse for Child Welfare, 2011a), but it includes interventions that are *promising* until proved ineffective or harmful (e.g., Alcoholics Anonymous [A.A.]) CEBC, 2011b).

As discussed in Chapter 2, the research and progress on evidence-based practice are also driven by the historical context of translational research with its focus on understanding and facilitating the translation of research to practice. That context is largely one of clinical research by biomedical scientists intent on "translating" products (usually pharmaceuticals) developed in controlled laboratory settings, often with animal models, into resources for use in real-world clinical environments. Part of the challenge of conducting translational research in social work is making it relevant to the context of social work research and practice, which share similarities to bench and bedside but which also possess features that distinguish them from clinical research, including a focus on social justice and definition of clients as individuals, groups, organizations, and communities.

Scientific Community and Research Evidence

At this point it is important to raise a set of questions: Why is the social work profession interested in better and more effective use of scientific evidence in social work practice? Why has the scientific community long been coming up short in delivering practice-pertinent evidence in an effective fashion? What is the background of this longstanding struggle to bridge social work research and social work practice?

One approach emanating from the philosophy of science might shed some important light on the research and practice gap dilemma: the research interest of the scientific community, especially in conjunction with the interest of the profession in social change.

Social workers and social work researchers define the scope of research on social work practice in broad terms to accommodate multiple core factors, including values, relationships, legislation, clinical experience, and organizations as fields of activity and research. Nevertheless, social work practice is very much about interventions. In other words, the core of social work practice is intervention for the betterment of clients, whether they are individuals, groups, or communities. From this perspective, it is easy to understand that the profession is in constant need of scientific evidence on the efficacy of various interventions, as well as evidence-based tools to deliver services that are safe, effective, cost-efficient, and expected to change the life situations of clients for the better. How is it, then, that the scientific community traditionally has not been able to respond to the needs of the profession?

In his remarkable book *Real Science: What It Is, and What It Means* (2000), John Ziman placed science in the complexity of value systems and politics to emphasize its social character. Ziman noted that, traditionally, scientific activity and production of evidence are discipline-based, and he made a distinction between fundamental and applied research. This inveterate characteristic of traditional science implies a distinction between core theoretical knowledge and other areas of knowledge such as social work "science," in which theoretical knowledge as well as empirical knowledge is translated into application (implementation). Many (or most) scientists are employed by universities with a specific culture and work environment that impose a set of rules and obligations upon them. Traditionally, academic environments tend to make their own rules and use public and private funds mostly independently in the name of academic freedom and scientific truth. For researchers, this is a challenging environment in which to work. Evaluated by their peers and expected to demonstrate increasing creativity, researchers develop strategies for survival and career advancement. Noncompliance with the guidelines of the academy is very costly. Scientists who do not play by the rules risk being left behind by funding institutions, universities, and their peers.

Generally, academic research environments are not open to practitioner and consumer input. Lack of such input manifests itself in the most critical ways when it comes to the production of, and access to, high-quality evidence for effective and better professional performance; this includes deficits in identifying research questions with a high degree of relevance for frontline social work, lack of practitioner and consumer interest in understanding scientific data, and, most seriously, deficits in translating research results to the benefit of end users. In a closed system where research and practice travel their relative trajectories without collaborative transactions, the ability of research communities to meet the needs of the profession will be very limited.

Fortunately for the human services professions, the divide between research and practice has been challenged for the past 20 years or so in two directions. Opening up research and practice for mutually beneficial transactions has developed both top-down and bottom-up.

The top-down developments are a result of the interest and initiatives of national and international governments and private institutions to promote better and more cost-efficient human services to end users. Professional organizations and consumer group networks are also supportive of such initiatives. A series of events has revitalized awareness within the scientific communities and human services professions of the importance of translational research. These events include the development of the science and technology of systematic research reviews by the Cochrane and Campbell collaborations, a global evidence-based movement in health (evidence-based medicine, EBM) and human (EBP) services. Also included are emerging high-quality clearinghouses that disseminate information on evidence-based interventions in plain language, increasing accessibility to audiences such as professional groups, clients, patients, and families of those who need support. Thanks to these and other developments, an increasing number of scientists, professionals such as social workers, decision makers, and end users of health and human services became, and are increasingly becoming, aware of the importance of high-quality evidence in support of interventions. Government initiatives in many countries to promote better and more accessible evidence for end users have become powerful mechanisms of supporting social work and other human services. For instance, as we will see in the following chapters, some of the cutting-edge projects on translational and implementation research are funded by the National Institutes of Health, a research funding infrastructure in the U.S. government. The California Evidence-Based Clearinghouse for Child Welfare, a global leader in this field, is funded by the state of California. The international Campbell Collaboration is currently funded by the government of Norway, and so on.

Although it is not completely detached from top-down initiatives, there is a bottom-up development as well. In 1994, Gibbons and colleagues published *The New Production of Knowledge: The Dynamics of Science and Research in Contemporary Societies,* a book describing the emergence of a new mode of knowledge production compared with the traditional disciplinary production of knowledge. The new mode is characterized by organizational diversity; research might be organized by independent research centers, government agencies, think tanks, practice-based units, and so on. Furthermore, it is characterized by practical problem orientation, transdisciplinarity, social accountability, and quality control involving all stakeholders and not just the academic community. Problem orientation relates directly to problem solving in the context of professional practice, and not necessarily in response to theoretical demands of a specific scientific discipline. Transdisciplinarity brings in multiple components to promote practice-pertinent and applicable knowledge: The research *problem* is solved in the practice context, the research *process* is focused on problem solution—although solutions to the problem may come with theoretical insights to satisfy disciplinary requirements—and the research *results* are directly transferred to the end user during the research process and immediately after the project conclusion. Researchers are accountable to the practitioners and other stakeholders. This research mode produces evidence in a primarily single setting, even if, at times, research results may be pertinent to other contexts.

Translational and Implementation Research Defined

Translational research is defined here as the study of the process of applying ideas, insights, and discoveries generated through basic scientific inquiry to the treatment or prevention of human disease and improvement of individual and social welfare, as illustrated in a figure adapted from one contained in a recent Institute of Medicine Report (O'Connell, Boat, & Warner, 2009) (Figure 1.1). In other words, translational research seeks to explain and facilitate the process of research translation. Although research translation may be said to actually begin at the preintervention stage, in this book we focus on the phases of the process labeled *effectiveness, dissemination,* and *implementation.* The aims of translational research are (1) to assess the effectiveness of an intervention or evidence-based practice in a real-world setting in achieving a specific set of outcomes (effectiveness); (2) to assess and contribute to the distribution of information and intervention materials to a specific social work, public health, or clinical practice audience (dissemination); and (3) to assess and potentially facilitate or promote its adoption, use, and sustainability in such settings (implementation) (Proctor et al., 2009).

Implementation is defined as a purposefully designed set of actions for the application of a purposefully designed program or intervention to cause change. *Implementation research* is defined as the "study of processes and strategies that move, or integrate, evidence-based effective treatments into routine use, in usual care settings" (Proctor et al., 2009, p. 27). Along with effectiveness and dissemination research, implementation research represents one

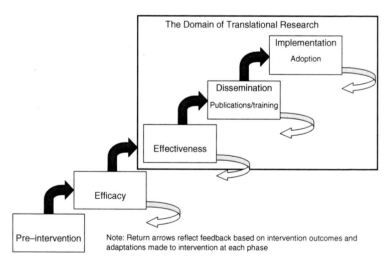

FIGURE 1.1 *Phases of Research Translation and Domain of Translational Research*

form of translational research and one stage or component of the process of research translation.

Importance of Translation

The purpose of studies of social work interventions is to understand the impact of the interventions on clients. Scientific evidence of what works is always an *estimate* of the impact of intervention variables on outcome variables. In a study of any given research question, the ultimate purpose of the scientific inquiry is to generalize knowledge from particular cases to an estimate that might help understand other populations that were not studied. The classic methodologic notion of external validity is about testing whether a scientific result that is valid in one context is also valid in another context. The stronger the external validity, then the stronger is the probability that a scientific estimate would be applicable in other contexts. However, even if an estimate is associated with higher external validity, such results are still estimates. Scientific estimates pose the problem that it is impossible to know the truth in any given research question with complete certainty (Soydan, 2008).

When using scientific evidence in social work interventions, there will always be a degree of uncertainty about the outcomes of any intervention. Therefore, translating generalized evidence to particular contexts, whether it is a single client, a group of clients, or a community, becomes important and necessary to strengthen the probability of successful implementation. As the coming chapters in this book will illustrate, however, translational research is more than simply conducting research about the process of translation; it is also about translating, adapting, and tailoring generalized evidence (evidence-based interventions) for implementation in contexts where the evidence-based interventions were not previously tested. Such translational research, given that a satisfactory degree of program integrity is maintained during the process of implementation, is also a generator of external validity.

Translation of generalized evidence to specific new contexts is similar to the mission of *evidence-based practice* (EBP) when it is defined as a *process*. The *products* of this process are often referred to as evidence-based practices, evidence-based interventions, or evidence-based treatments. Originally, EBP was developed as a model for medical practice. Originators of EBP defined it, purposefully, as "the conscientious, explicit and judicious use of current best evidence in making decisions about the care of individual patients" (Sackett, Richardson, Rosenberg, & Haynes, 1997, p. 2). The term "current best evidence" is the most explicit expression of the recognition that we cannot know with certainty the level of efficacy and effectiveness of a given intervention, and thus the "gold standard" of evidence emphasized by the Cochrane and Campbell collaborations, individual research institutions, and researchers is unattainable. But "current best evidence" also alludes to the fact that in intervening professions, notably in social work, many interventions may not have a body of research, and especially not research results obtained by randomized controlled studies, to support what works. A further complication is that the robustness of the evidence may vary depending on outcome variables, diverse subgroups of a client population, context of the intervention, and the condition for which it is implemented. Therefore, the original developers of evidence-based medicine integrated three fundamental factors to form the framework of EBP: current best evidence, physicians' professional expertise, and patients' predicaments, rights, and preferences. This basic model was later transported to other fields of human services, including social work practice. Now a classic definition in social work, it was reorganized as a seven-step process model (Gibbs, 2003):

- Step 1—Become motivated to apply EBP.
- Step 2—Convert information need into an answerable question.
- Step 3—Track down best available evidence to answer the question.
- Step 4—Appraise the evidence critically.
- Step 5—Integrate evidence with practice experience and characteristics of client or situation.

- Step 6—Evaluate effectiveness and efficiency in exercising the steps.
- Step 7—Teach others to do the same.

Currently, EBP is viewed as a work process and translational research as an effort to understand the best ways of bringing evidence to practice follow different, historically contingent, developmental trajectories. However, a new attempt to integrate the translational science and research on EBP might emerge in the future. Conceptually integrated empirical studies of EBP and translation and implementation processes in human services seem feasible and should be considered.

Social Workers as Researchers of Translation of Evidence-Based Interventions

The utilization of best available scientific evidence on what works in social work places social workers in a unique position; they are expected to evaluate the effectiveness of their own methods in the process of performing EBP. Social work professionals do not have a strong tradition of conducting systematic evaluations of their own practice. Health care practitioners, especially medical doctors, in teaching and training health care settings have longstanding experience with integrating practice, scientific investigation, and teaching. With a serious introduction of translational and implementation approaches into social work practice, social workers will increasingly find themselves in a position in which expectations for participation in translation and effective implementation will become an imperative. So, what factors would nourish such an environment?

First, similar to health care professionals, social workers encounter clients directly (e.g., face-to-face, telephone calls, letters, etc.) in defined organizational settings such as social services agencies, mental health clinics, neighborhoods, and communities. Direct contact between social workers and clients provides a context in which outcomes of evidence-based interventions can be studied.

Organizational settings of social work practice are propitious venues for methodically observing, registering, and systematizing data on client outcomes and other circumstances associated with the impact of professional practice.

Second, social work has a broad practice field. Social workers operate in diverse settings, including social work agencies, health and mental health settings, schools, prisons, workplaces, communities, and international venues. This means there is access to and personal experience of environments representing almost all settings in our societies where evidence-based interventions can be developed and evidence-based services can be delivered.

Third, social work practice involves all aspects of human and societal interaction. From micro to mezzo to macro, social workers confront a host of psychological, sociopsychological, cognitive, and community-based problems. Translation is inherently a phenomenon of social interaction.

Fourth, the nature of the social work profession demands that social workers be both culture brokers and change agents in working with individual clients, families, and communities. While seeking to transform societies and the lives of individual members of societies, social workers are also in a unique position to exercise leadership in brokering the organizational cultures of the researcher and the practitioner and facilitating change in practice (Palinkas, 2010).

Circumstances such as those mentioned earlier are factors that encourage social worker participation in translational and implementation research. Now that EBP is gaining considerable momentum in an increasing number of countries, social work has the opportunity to take a leading role in translational science. Yet, the profession needs to contribute to building an infrastructure for the effective translation and implementation of evidence-based interventions. Some of the chapters in this book describe partnerships and strategies in which social work is involved. What is needed in the future is the identification and sustainable establishment of favorable research infrastructures promoting the unique opportunity for social workers to substantially contribute to translational research.

The Structure of the Book

The objective in Chapter 2 is to introduce and explain the concepts of evidence-based practice as product, EBP as process, translation, dissemination, and implementation. This chapter provides a necessary and useful conceptual framework on which to understand the aims, issues, and background of translational and implementation research, and it examines the operation of basic concepts within the discipline and practice of social work and its core mission to promote social justice, focus on the person in environment, and work on behalf of vulnerable and disenfranchised groups.

In Chapter 3 we provide a more detailed examination of translational research by highlighting its role in understanding and facilitating the process of EBP implementation. The chapter is divided into two sections. The first section presents examples of studies of evidence-based practice effectiveness, dissemination, and implementation within the context of social work practice. The second section of the chapter provides a more detailed examination of research on evidence-based practice implementation. This section reviews studies conducted by social workers and/or in social work practice settings of barriers to and facilitators of EBP implementation, and the development and evaluation of evidence-based "strategies" designed to overcome these barriers and facilitate implementation.

In Chapter 4, we examine the process and outcomes of EBP translation and implementation as an integrated focus of translational research. We introduce the principles and practice of research on EBP translation and implementation process and outcomes and provide examples of research projects and activities that have focused on either one or both of these aspects of translation and implementation. The chapter also touches on challenges inherent to conducting translational research and offers strategies to address those issues. To further illustrate the concepts discussed in the chapter, we also present a case study of two related projects that examined process and outcomes of a randomized controlled trial of the effectiveness of an evidence-based practice in child welfare settings.

Chapter 5 is dedicated to studying organizational settings as the locus of EBP and examining the stages of translation from the perspective of both the researcher and the human services agency. In this chapter we draw upon the literature of organizational theory to examine how human service organizations function, how and why they resist innovative practices, and how they come to accept innovation and adapt to the demands of the new practice. We also introduce the principles and practice of research on organizational culture and climate and provide examples of research projects and activities that have focused on the influence of organizational factors on the translation and implementation in social work practice. Several case examples, including the statewide implementation of SafeCare®, designed to prevent child maltreatment and reduce the need for out-of-home placements in child welfare in Oklahoma, illustrate the challenges and infrastructural requirements of organization-level research.

In Chapter 6, the mixed-methods approach to understanding the process, context, and outcomes of translating research into practice is brought into focus. We introduce the principles and practice of mixed methods and provide examples of translational research projects and activities that incorporate different mixed-methods designs. These examples—along with a case study of evidence-based intervention translation in a social work practice setting (community mental health clinics)—illustrate how the use of such designs can address some of the challenges to conducting research on EBP translation and implementation introduced in Chapters 4 and 5. We conclude with a discussion of the infrastructure requirements to support mixed-method research, including training in methods, data collection, and data analysis.

Our attention to methodologic issues continues in Chapter 7. This chapter begins with an introduction of the principles and practice of community-based participatory research and examples of research projects and activities where the community has served as a "natural laboratory" for translational research. The chapter also includes a case study of Communities That Care, a prevention service delivery system that involves the use of academic–community partnerships to conduct translational research on effectiveness and implementation of evidence-based practices to prevent adolescent health and behavior problems. This case study describes the development of strategies for academic and clinician engagement in community-based participatory research to facilitate the adoption, implementation, and use of different evidence-based health and social service interventions. These examples illustrate how the development of community–research partnerships can address some of the challenges of conducting translational research. We conclude with a discussion of the infrastructure required to support community-based participatory research.

Chapter 8 summarizes the main themes introduced in this book and reflects on future steps in the field. It suggests opportunities for conducting research on EBP translation and implementation that are based on the research strategy described in the book and are consistent with the core mission and values of the field of social work. It presents an argument for the importance of such a strategy in conducting research that will both understand and support the movement of EBP from effectiveness to dissemination to implementation to sustainability. It concludes with a summary of the infrastructure requirements for conducting such research within the field of social work.

Because this book is one of a series of books on research methods in social work, it is intended to offer guidance to researchers and practitioners on how to conduct translational research. It is not a guide on how to translate research, although translational research is a necessary element of research translation, as noted earlier. Furthermore, we have introduced case studies and other examples throughout the book of translational research conducted by social workers (those holding an master's degree or doctorate in social work), by non–social workers based in schools of social work, or in social work practice settings. Translational research is inherently interdisciplinary and benefits from contributions made by scholars in several fields of inquiry; thus, we thought it best not to limit our focus to research conducted by social workers.

Additional Resources

For more information on translational science:

Brekke, J. S., Ell, K., & Palinkas, L. A. (2007). Translational science at the National Institute of Mental Health: Can social work take its rightful place? *Research on Social Work Practice, 17*(1), 123–33. doi: 10.1177/1049731506293693

Michie, S., Fixsen, D., Grimshaw, J. M., & Eccles, M. P. (2009). Specifying and reporting complex behaviour change interventions: The need for a scientific method. *Implementation Science, 4*(40). doi: 10.1186/1748-5908-4-40

2

Translation and Implementation of Evidence-Based Practices

The translation and implementation of evidence-based practices involve a number of interrelated concepts. In this chapter, the aim is to contextualize the main concepts used in this book. Translation and implementation of evidence-based practices take place in a context of evidence production, innovation diffusion, and dissemination. Our intent here is to describe some of the complexities of this context.

Sources of Research Evidence

There is some confusion in the social work profession in terms of defining "evidence-based practice" and EBP. Although the phrase is frequently used to refer to an "evidence-supported intervention" or "evidence-supported treatment," it is important to note that the term "evidence-based practice" is also defined as a process model. In this book whenever the term is used in referring to a process, the acronym "EBP" will be used. EBP is a professional culture. The process of EBP occurs through a series of interactions between professionals, clients, and other stakeholders, such as clients' families. The core of the professional culture, or the state of mind, is the professional's ability to identify the client system deficits, access and assess the best possible research evidence, and use this evidence to eliminate deficits in the specific context of client values, culture, and preferences, in addition to identifying the opportunities and constraints generated by the context of the human services organizations. In this section, we focus on one component of EBP: namely, research evidence on what works and what is potentially harmful in social work practice. During the course of developing EBP, proponents have established a consensus on the merit and value of different types of evidence. This consensus is reflected in the form of a conceptual frame of reference that arranges different types of evidence resources in a hierarchy. In very general terms, the hierarchy of evidence is based on the ability of different types of research designs to control for and, if possible, eliminate various types of biases that dilute estimates of the efficacy and effectiveness of social interventions. Furthermore, the quality (robustness) of scientific evidence is contingent on how well a research process was performed. For example, although randomized controlled experimental trial (RCT) designs are superior to quasi-experimental (nonrandomized) designs, a well-conducted and statistically powerful quasi-experimental study might yield higher-quality, stronger scientific evidence than an RCT that was poorly conducted with low statistical power. In addition to evidence strength, effective interventions must have relevance to social work problems; often, the effectiveness of interventions is limited to specific client groups, to specific problems, and to certain circumstances.

In the following section, we describe two main types of evidence sources: (1) traditional scientific formats including primary research and synthesis of primary research (systematic research reviews) and (2) repackaged scientific evidence for dissemination by clearinghouses and other organizations as practice guidelines and other types of databases.

Primary Research

The traditional source of evidence is primary research. Since the establishment of social science rules governing empirical research processes, primary research has been, and still is, the basic source of scientific evidence. Questions addressed through primary research seem to be endless, continuously generated by human needs and curiosity. Nowadays, primary empirical research offers a broad spectrum of research tools from which to choose. Different empirical research tools, or research designs, are appropriate and effective for different types of research questions. In other words, once a research question is formulated and deemed researchable, the researcher should choose the best research design to investigate that specific question.

In evidence-based social work practice, the primary research (and practice) interest is to understand whether an intervention, program, or policy works, for whom it works, and under what circumstances it works. Preference is usually given to quantitative and, in particular, experimental research designs to achieve this understanding. But not all questions are related to effectiveness in EBP. Many issues pertaining to EBP require application of nonquantitative (i.e., qualitative) and nonexperimental designs. Here are a few examples to illustrate an important research aspect of EBP—that social work interventions are implemented with the purpose of improving negative and undesirable life situations. For example, parent-child interaction therapy (PCIT) is designed to generate safety and child/family well-being by addressing issues of emotional abuse, physical abuse, and physical neglect. Understanding the effectiveness of PCIT for children and parents involved in maltreatment requires an experimental design approach. On the other hand, if we are interested in understanding the circumstances that facilitate or inhibit the effectiveness, dissemination, or use of PCIT with African American children in the foster care system, it would be wise to apply nonexperimental—observational (quantitative) or process study (qualitative)—research designs. Furthermore, understanding client values and acceptance of interventions is vital to successful EBP. In such cases, qualitative research designs would be most effective. With this broad view of scientific methods of inquiry in mind, let's take a closer look at different types of methodologies used by social work researchers to understand the effects of social work interventions.

Randomized Controlled Experiments

When studying the impact of social work interventions, the research design that generates the least-biased estimates is the randomized controlled experiment, or RCT. In RCTs of social work interventions, eligible clients or entities such as mental health clinics, social services districts, neighborhoods, and communities are randomly allocated to one of two or more treatment conditions. The treatment conditions may be a social work intervention program and a nontreatment control group. One or more social work intervention programs may be tested in a single study. Groups that are constructed by random allocation do not differ systematically. However, they may differ by chance. RCTs, when conducted properly with sufficiently large samples for strong statistical analysis, generate the best possible or least-biased estimates of the effects of social work interventions. However, it is not always possible to conduct controlled experiments. Alternative designs to RCTs are known as quasi-experimental studies.

In the study of social work interventions, the use of RCTs may be associated with barriers that create serious problems for application. Such barriers include ineligibility of multiproblem clients, client dropout, difficulty controlling the experimental environment, client reluctance to enroll, and ethical issues related to the well-being of the client.

Quasi-experimental Research Designs

The term "quasi-experimental research design" is an umbrella name for various types of studies that are considered experimental but do not use the random assignment of subjects. Quasi-experimental research designs are used for a number of reasons, including practical problems of implementation, ethical concerns, budget and time restrictions, or unwillingness of providers or consumers to participate in RCTs. These designs include the *controlled clinical trial* (CCT), in which participants (or other units) are definitely assigned prospectively to one or two (or more) alternative forms of intervention using a quasi-random allocation method (e.g., alternation, date of birth, patient identifier) or possibly assigned prospectively to one or two (or more) alternative forms of intervention using a process of random or quasi-random allocation; the *controlled before and after study* (CBA), in which intervention and control groups are defined other than by random process, and a baseline period of assessment of main outcomes is included; and the *interrupted time series* (ITS), in which a change in trend is attributable to the intervention (Cochrane Effective Practice and Organisation of Care Review Group, 2002). Models generated by mathematical (re)constructions are also examples of quasi-experimental designs.

Because experimental study designs, with or without random allocation of subjects, are considered the best possible designs for studying the effects of social interventions, researchers have made efforts to understand differences between randomized and nonrandomized designs in terms of biases that blur the results produced by these designs. To understand the differences of bias produced by randomized controlled experiments with those of quasi-experimental designs, researchers use "between-study" and "within-study" comparisons.

In between-study comparisons, researchers examine multiple studies conducted with different research designs. The bias is calculated by studying the relationship between the design and the estimates of effect; Reynolds and Temple (1995) compared three studies, Shadish and Ragsdale (1996) compared dozens of studies, and Lipsey and Wilson (1993) compared 74 randomized and nonrandomized studies to understand how close the estimates of nonrandomized designs come to the estimates of randomized design studies. All of these studies show mixed results. A major problem with these types of studies is that one cannot distinguish whether the difference between estimates is a result of the design or of some other factor (Glazerman, Levy, & Myers, 2003).

Within-study comparisons examine an intervention program's effect by using a randomized control group and one or several nonrandomized comparison groups. These studies use design replication as a method, which is a reestimation of the effect by using one or several comparison groups. These types of studies are capable of showing that the estimated differences between randomized and nonexperimental study designs are due to the differences in design, and not to other factors such as investigator bias, differences in treatment environments, or implementation itself. Glazerman and colleagues (2003) conducted a within-study comparison of 12 labor market–related studies. They found that quasi-experimentally measured estimates sometimes came close to replicating experimentally generated results but often produced estimates that differed with margins of importance for policy making. This is considered an estimate of bias. The researchers concluded that "although the empirical evidence from this literature can be used in the context of training and welfare programs to *improve* non-experimental research designs, it cannot on its own justify the use of such designs" (Glazerman et al., 2003, p. 63). Boruch (2007) also offers a thoughtful account of this problem.

Observational Study Designs

When it is not possible to use randomized controlled studies and quasi-experimental studies with less vulnerability to selection bias, researchers turn to observational studies. An observational study is a study in which variables of interest are observed rather than manipulated. "Observational study design" is an umbrella term for a variety of research designs. Correlational studies, single-case designs, and some other bias-heavy designs—such as pretest–posttest studies without control groups, anecdotal case studies, and qualitative studies—are classified as observational studies. In some literature, even quasi-experimental studies are included in this category. Single-case or single-system designs are studies of a client or a group of clients over a long time with observation repeated at several intervals. These designs generate data about the subject's conditions, such as during a treatment period.

Although observational studies are considered inferior to the gold standard of RCTs, there are circumstances when they may produce more rigorous results or results similar to those of RCTs at less cost. For instance, a review of 99 articles representing five different clinical areas revealed that the findings of observational studies were remarkably similar to those of RCTs (Concato, Shah, & Horwitz, 2000).

However, the issue of bias in an estimate of the effects of an intervention program remains controversial. Summarizing the latest literature on this topic, Soydan (2008) notes that although nonexperimental estimates of the effects of interventions may, at times, come close to results estimated with RCTs, the problem of bias remains and threatens practice and policy decisions.

Limitations of Primary Research

Although primary research creates the foundation of our knowledge base, its use in translation efforts is associated with a number of problems. First, there is the general problem of the time gap between the publication of a scientific work reporting a new innovation (e.g., an evidence-based intervention) and its utilization in practice. As noted in Chapter 1, this gap may be as long as 20 years. Green and colleagues conceptualized this gap between the production and transfer of knowledge from research to practice as a pipeline in which the vetting of the research through successive screens ensures the quality of the research that is delivered to practitioners and policy makers but does little to ensure the relevance and fit of that research to the needs, circumstances, and populations of those practice or policy applications (Green, Ottoson, Garcia, & Hiatt, 2009).

Second, the issue of information overload has been around for a long time and the overload continues to grow. For example, there are already more than 15 million medical articles, including articles on mental health. The number of journals that solely publish summaries of articles published in other journals is more than 250 (Greenhalgh, 2001, p. 15). There are nearly 7,000 open access journals (http://www.doaj.org; accessed February 20, 2011). The overload problem overwhelms researchers, professional practitioners, and others interested in evidence-based innovations that can be translated for use in different contexts.

Third, the inconsistency of scientific research is a very common problem. Everyone versed in current events knows that scientists are constantly making discoveries that challenge assumed "truths" about health and wellness; anything that was good for health yesterday might be declared bad for health today! This is very confusing to all users of scientific evidence.

Fourth, given that readers can access all pertinent publications, the quality control of studies is a painstaking process and does not render itself to easy handling by individuals. This problem has been demonstrated by the work of the Cochrane and Campbell collaborations (more is given on the collaborations later). In the development of systematic research reviews, including meta-analysis of effectiveness studies, these collaborations have relied on rigorous methods of controlling the scientific quality of published and unpublished scientific material. In all likelihood, no more than 10% to 15% of the material appraised by these collaborations has lasting scientific value and qualifies for inclusion in the gold standard systematic research reviews.

In sum, primary research is the foundation of our knowledge base, but it is associated with fundamental and serious problems that make the use of cutting-edge innovations difficult and risky in the context of evidence translation for practice. This brings us to research reviews and systematic research reviews.

Research Reviews

Research reviews have long been an instrument of summarizing large chunks of research results. Prior to research reviews, social scientists would conduct "discourse" analysis, which is a summary and critique of views, thoughts, and facts in a specific field. Today, discourse analysis is limited to theoretical conversations in the social sciences, while a research review is used when empirical research results are involved. Traditionally, such reviews have been prepared by high-profile researchers and experts in specific topic areas. However, high scientific prestige may not be a good indicator of the quality of scientific evidence reviews. Petticrew and Roberts (2006) report several examples of biased literature reviews that misled other experts and the public. Their example of the case of vitamin C as a preventive intervention illustrates the fallacy of traditional research reviews. In 1986, Nobel Laureate Linus Pauling published a book that reviewed the extensive literature on the merit of vitamin C in preventing the occurrence of the common cold. Pauling concluded that large amounts of vitamin C prevented the cold, but it turned out that his research review was nonsystematic. Some years later, Paul Knipschild (1994) conducted a systematic research review involving an exhaustive search of pertinent databases, including a manual search of both unpublished and published but not database-indexed literature. He found 61 trials, of which 15 passed the strict methodological standards set by the reviewers. On the basis of the literature, Knipschild concluded that not even massive doses of vitamin C could prevent a cold. He also found that 5 of the 15 qualified trials, as well as two other studies, were not mentioned by Pauling. Unfortunately, a careful appraisal of social work and other journals may reveal articles subtitled "A research review" that are conducted without a systematic approach, lack an adequate description of the method as to blur transparency, and do not adhere to high scientific standards.

Systematic Research Reviews

The notion of systematic research review was originally developed by researchers affiliated with the Cochrane Collaboration (http://www.cochrane.org), a nonprofit organization focused on health- and mental health–related sciences and practices, and later adopted and adapted by the founders of the Campbell Collaboration (http://www.campbellcollaboration.org), which focuses on social sciences and human services. A systematic research review is a synthesis of all empirical evidence that matches a set of eligibility criteria and aims to answer a specified research question. Systematic research reviews must use explicit, transparent, and systematic methods to identify, block, or eliminate all types of biases that may be involved in the process of preparing such a review. Whenever possible, systematic research reviews include a "meta-analysis," which is an umbrella term for statistically synthesizing estimates (effect sizes) of multiple randomized or quasi-randomized effectiveness studies. The Cochrane and Campbell collaborations define the core characteristics of systematic research reviews as follows:

- Clearly stated set of objectives with predefined eligibility criteria for studies
- Explicit, reproducible methodology
- Systematic search that attempts to identify all studies that would meet the eligibility criteria
- Assessment of the validity of the findings of the included studies, such as through the assessment of risk of bias
- Systematic presentation, and synthesis, of the characteristics and findings of the included studies (Higgins & Green, 2008)

Systematic research reviews by the collaborations are available online or in CD-based libraries. The reviews are detailed, explicit, and transparent accounts of the scientific process through which each review was prepared, and the contents of the reviews include the results and conclusions of the reviewers. However, these highly technical reports—which often demand some degree of familiarity with the terminology of systematic research reviews—also include a two-page, plain-language description of the review, providing an easy reading experience to end users who are not familiar with scientific terminology.

Development of systematic research reviews was driven by a number of factors. As mentioned, information overload and related problems of accessing and appraising the quality of primary studies have been major factors. Another factor is dissatisfaction with the deficits of traditional research reviews that lead to inaccurate or invalid conclusions. Furthermore, and perhaps foremost, there is an increasing awareness among end users of the need for high-quality evidence for effective, transparent, and high-quality interventions. An example of a systematic research review of the intervention "Scared Straight" is provided in the following box.

Campbell Collaboration Research Review
Policy Brief—November 28, 2003

Does taking juveniles on tours of prison deter them from future crime and delinquency?

The Policy Question

A recent Illinois law mandates the Chicago Public Schools to identify children at risk for future criminal behavior and take them on tours of adult prison facilities. The law revisits the long history of using programs like "Scared Straight," which involve organized visits to prison facilities by juvenile delinquents or children at risk for becoming delinquent. The programs are designed to deter participants from future offending by providing first-hand observations of prison life and interaction with adult inmates. Do they work to reduce crime and delinquency by participants?

Results of the Campbell Collaboration Review

Results of this review indicate that not only does it fail to deter crime but it actually leads to more offending behavior. Government officials permitting this program need to adopt rigorous evaluation to ensure that they are not causing more harm to the very citizens they pledge to protect.

Methods

Review authors conducted a vigorous search for randomized [or seemingly randomized] studies evaluating the effects of Scared Straight or similar programs on subsequent offending. They located nine randomized studies, in which seven provided outcome data making it possible to include them in a quantitative procedure known as meta-analysis. It was only possible to do this for the "first post-treatment effect," as most studies did not report measurements at subsequent time intervals. Unfortunately, little information on incidence, severity and latency measures was provided, so the meta-analysis was completed on prevalence data only (the proportion of each group that failed or succeeded).

In the graph below [(Table 2.1)], the seven studies used in the meta-analysis are analyzed and plotted using a "Forrest Graph." The study's author(s) are provided in the left column, followed by the number of participants who were arrested (or committed a new offense) compared to their total number for treatment and control groups. Treatment groups received Scared Straight or a similar program while control groups did not receive the intervention. The important thing in the graph is that odds ratios larger than "1" favor the control group while odds ratios lower than "1" favor the experimental group. In nearly all of the studies, the odds ratios favor the control groups, and the overall meta-analysis is negative for the program (Petrosino, Turpin-Petrosino, & Buehler, 2004).

Table 2.1 in the facing page

TABLE 2.1. Petrosino et al. Report Findings

Study	Treatment n/N	Control n/N	OR (95%CI Random)	Weight %	OR (95% CI Random)
Finckenauer 1982	19/46	4/35		9.8	5.43 (1.65, 18.02)
GERP & DC 1979	16/94	8/67		14.7	1.51 (0.61, 3.77)
Lewis 1983	43/53	37/55		15.3	2.09 (0.86, 5.09)
Michigan D.O.C 1967	12/28	5/30		9.5	3.75 (1.11, 12.67)
Orchowsky & Taylor 1981	16/39	16/41		15.2	1.09 (0.44, 2.66)
Vreeland 1981	14/39	11/40		13.9	1.48 (0.57, 3.83)
Yarborough 1979	27/137	17/90		21.6	1.05 (0.54, 2.07)
Total (95% CI)	147/436	98/358		100.0	1.72 (1.13, 2.62)

Favours treatment   Favours control

Test for heterogeneity chi-square=8.50 df=6 p=0.2
Test for overall effect z=2.55 p=0.01

n, Number of participants re-offending; N, number assigned to group; OR, odds ratio; CI, confidence intervals; weight, amount of weight given to study in analysis.

In sum, systematic research reviews provide best available evidence on what works, what is promising, and what is potentially harmful in social work and other types of interventions. However, the number of systematic research reviews produced by the Cochrane and Campbell collaborations is still very limited. When there is no systematic research review on a specific knowledge and intervention topic, end users such as social workers will have to look for other sources of information. High-quality RCTs would provide the next best level of analysis in the hierarchy of evidence.

Repackaged Scientific Evidence for Dissemination

One specific type of knowledge source that has been introduced in recent years is known as a repackaged scientific information source. Research packaged for professional use, such as those programs promoted by professional organizations or made available on government websites, may have more accessible information about the specific implementation of evidence-based interventions and programs.

To bridge the gap between research and professional practice, some research results have been rendered in special formats and indicate what treatments or interventions work or are promising. The three most common types of packaged tools for translating evidence for implementation are (1) manual-based treatment packages, (2) best practice recommendations or guidelines, and (3) expert consensus guidelines. The foremost merit of research packaged for professional use, especially manual-based treatment, is that it has a high degree of transportability. These tools are tailored to make research results easily applicable in real-life situations, and they can be disseminated extensively to end users.

However, packaged research may not always rely on the highest-quality evidence available. There are a number of reasons why this occurs, including the following:

• Package developers may not always be aware of or look for high-quality evidence.

- Package developers may be biased by being either stakeholders or proponents of the package.
- Packages are often developed by researchers who conduct studies of their own intervention models.
- Some evidence indicates that when intervention model developers are also evaluators who "own" the intervention, research results tend to be inflated.

Social workers need to assess the evidence base of research packages by using critical thinking skills, applying the tools for finding credible and relevant research, and conducting independent assessments of packaged research-based interventions. Two good forms of independent assessment are high-quality efficacy studies conducted by independent researchers and high-quality systematic reviews.

Manuals, Best Practice Recommendations, and Expert Consensus Guidelines

Traditionally, manuals, best practice recommendations, and expert consensus guidelines have been mentioned as if they were the same or very similar instruments. In recent years, with the advance of the EBP know-how and techniques, these instruments have been reshaped and defined more adequately.

Manual-based treatments are intervention models that are marketed in a manual format that translates scientific evidence into real-life situations by using practical instructions. Best practice recommendations or guidelines are practical recommendations derived from systematic reviews of the literature on a clinical question by a panel of experts to assist practitioners in making sound clinical decisions. Expert consensus guidelines are specific recommendations for practice with a particular population based on a consensus of experts.

Manual-based treatments. Manuals are prepared to:

- Translate scientific evidence into easily accessible and implementation-friendly formats

- Provide clear, comprehensive, and practical instructions for how to implement an intervention model
- Maintain the integrity of the treatment, or program "fidelity"
- Provide training instructions for social workers and their instructors
- Provide treatment assessment devices

Comprehensive instructions in manuals include information such as:

- Description of target group(s)
- Treatment session structure
- Objective(s) of each session
- Activities of each session
- Duration of each session
- Postsession quick assessment tools
- Forms for record maintenance
- Handouts for clients

Best practice recommendations or guidelines. While manual-based treatments are specifically developed for professional implementation and might be supported with diverse degrees of evidence strength, best practice recommendations do not necessarily include all dimensions (e.g., detailed implementation instructions, training instructions) of manual-based treatment packages but rather tend to offer recommendations based on what is perceived to be the best possible evidence available. However, it would be wise to cross-check with multiple sources for optimal quality assurance in professional practice.

Best practice recommendations have their origins in expert consensus guidelines. Dissatisfaction with a lack of or little scientific evidence of expert consensus guidelines, growing insight into the value of systematic research reviews, and critical appraisal of the quality of published and unpublished research have stimulated the development and dissemination of best practice recommendations by a diverse range of organizations, networks, and numerous other resources around the world. However, best practice recommendation resources might differ in several aspects, including exhaustiveness of searches (including hand search of unpublished and published literature), assessment of the quality of studies, assessment of the strength of evidence available, fashion and language of imposing recommendations, and guidance in implementation.

Expert consensus guidelines. Typically, expert consensus guidelines are developed by reaching consensus among leading researchers and clinical experts. In terms of quality and strength of evidence associated with expert consensus guidelines, the reader should be aware that guidelines are based on opinions of experts and their (often selective) view of the evidence rather than on transparent and scientifically rigorous empirical evidence.

Prestigious networks and organizations such as the Centers for Disease Control and Prevention (CDC) (http://www.thecommunityguide.org), the Cochrane and Campbell collaborations, and the Oxford Center of Evidence-Based Medicine (http://www.cebm.net) rate expert consensus guidelines very low on their scales of evidence levels. For instance, the Psychguides.com website raises the question: "How valid are the expert opinions provided in these guidelines?" The response given is: "For now, the honest answer is that we simply don't know." The backdrop of this insecurity is that experts are often confronted with the most difficult clinical questions and lean on incomplete research information. So why is expert opinion used if the evidence base of expert consensus guidelines is weak? Psychguides.com argues that expert consensus guidelines are needed because:

- Most research studies are difficult to generalize to everyday clinical practice
- Available controlled experiments and other empirical studies do not, and cannot possibly, address all the variations that arise in clinical practice
- Changes in the accepted best clinical practice often take place at a much faster rate than the necessarily slower-paced research efforts that would eventually provide scientific documentation for the change

An instructor might refer students to the Expert Consensus Guideline Series in mental disorders (http://www.psychguides. com). At this site, a number of guidelines can be studied as cases and compared to other evidence that might be retrieved from other, more dependable sources.

The National Guidelines Clearinghouse (http://www.guidelines. gov), operated by the Agency for Healthcare Research and Quality of the U.S. Department of Health and Human Services, is a very comprehensive database offering access to a large number of clinical practice guidelines on a variety of subjects. The site provides guidelines at their face value without indicating any assessment of the quality criteria and evidence levels used by individual guidelines. Unfortunately, diverse guideline developers do not always provide explicit details about the quality criteria that were used.

High-Quality Clearinghouses

As described, the Cochrane and Campbell collaborations are two leading producers and disseminators of high-quality evidence on what works in medicine and human services. These networks limit their work to collating evidence that fits predetermined standards and distribute this information in electronic (and CD-based) media. However, how efficiently and to what extent this evidence is used by end users such as physicians, nurses, social workers, school teachers, police, or the general public are largely unknown. Concerns about the limitations of translating evidence on what works into real-life situations led to the formation of more sophisticated forms of clearinghouses that are tailored to meet the needs of specific professions that serve specific populations. Good examples are the California Evidence-Based Clearinghouse for Child Welfare (http:// www.cebc4cw.org) run by the Chadwick Center for Children and Families; the Community Guide (http://www.thecommunityguide. org/index.html) run by the CDC; the Evidence-Based Database on Aging Care (http://www.searchedac.org) run by the New York Academy of Medicine's Social Work Leadership Institute; the

"Metodguide för Socialt Arbete" [Methodological Guide for Social Work] (http://www.socialstyrelsen.se/evidensbaseradpraktik) run by Sweden's National Board of Health and Welfare; and the Oxford Center of Evidence-Based Medicine (http://www.cebm.net). Although there are variations, these and other clearinghouses often provide information about evidence quality and the strength by which interventions are supported, their relevance to the specific problem or client group, alternative evidence-based interventions, descriptive information on accessibility, associated training and implementation costs, and other issues. Clearinghouses tend to track best available evidence such as systematic research reviews and, in their absence, good-quality RCTs to support interventions. Beyond these sources, and to some extent beyond high-quality quasi-experiments, the quality and strength of evidence on what works increasingly diminish.

In sum, there are excellent sources available to support translation efforts. In terms of content, there are limitations to and gaps in addressing all problems and issues that are faced by professionals and professional agencies. High-quality and well-organized clearinghouses provide invaluable information. The Cochrane and Campbell electronic libraries are excellent sources when they have what end users are looking for. High-quality randomized and quasi-randomized studies form the backbone of our knowledge base, but they are challenging sources in terms of accessing, appraising, and understanding the language.

Brief History of Approaches to Translate Research Results to End Users

Research evidence does not automatically reach practitioners or end users because the evidence was produced within communities of knowledge production. Translation and implementation of evidence presuppose processes of diffusion and dissemination. Everett Rogers, a leader in innovation theory and practice research, provides a history of diffusion research in his book *Diffusion of Innovations* (2003).

The roots of diffusion research go back to the early 1900s with the Frenchman Gabriel Tarde and the German Georg Simmel, both early leading sociologists. Tarde interpreted diffusion as a sociological process of social change, identified the importance of opinion leadership, and developed the S-shaped curve of cumulative adoptions (he used the term "imitation" rather than "adoption") over time. Tarde and Simmel both perceived adoption of innovations as processes of interpersonal communication networks. James Dearing (2008) notes that a 1943 article by Bryce Ryan and Neal Gross, who were interested in the diffusion of agricultural innovation, heavily affected future studies of innovation diffusion by pointing out key factors of successful innovation that emphasized individuals as the main factor of change. The importance of a centralized agency with change agents, effective communication channels, and an interest in adoption became core elements of innovation research. Innovation diffusion research spread from agricultural studies and practice to several other areas such as medical sociology, general sociology, education, organizational studies, public health, and, notably, marketing. Rogers, who started out in the field of agriculture, first published his milestone book, *Diffusion of Innovations,* in 1962. He identified five factors that impact the pace and rate of adoption of innovations (Rogers, 2003, pp. 15–16). The first of these factors, *relative advantage,* refers to the individual's need to understand whether an innovation brings about any advantages and betterment compared to the current means of action. For example, if social workers perceive the relative advantage of evidence-based practices, they will more often abandon opinion-based practices. So, the greater the perceived relative advantage of any innovation, the faster adoption will take place.

Rogers used the term *compatibility* to refer to the consistency between the innovation and the context of the existing needs, values, and experiences of the adopters. *Complexity* of an innovation refers to the extent to which an innovation is perceived as difficult to understand and use. Innovations with less complexity tend to be adopted faster and earlier because they are easier to understand and often include easily acquired skills.

Adoption of an innovation may be rapid if the potential adopters have a chance to try the innovation on a limited and temporary basis rather than on full scale. Rogers coined the term *trialability* to define this factor.

Finally, *observability* refers to the degree to which an innovation is visible to others. When results of adoption of a social work innovation are more visible in the network of social work agencies, more agencies will adopt the innovation (Rogers, 2003, pp. 15–16).

Rogers gave a broad definition of diffusion as the communication of an innovation through different channels over time to individuals of a certain social system. Referencing the Ryan and Gross 1943 data on adoption of hybrid seed corn by Iowa farmers, Rogers created the S-curve model to describe the formation of successful innovation adaptations. The S-curve suggests a normal distribution of innovation diffusion with few "early adopters" increasing slowly in the beginning of the diffusion process, followed by half of the adopters adopting the innovation rapidly. The curve tails off with a period of "late adopters" who gradually use the innovation.

Besides the key elements of the *innovation* as just described, the classic diffusion model includes the following components. The *adopter* is the individual who adopts an innovation. The adopter's degree of innovativeness is the attribute that affects the process of adoption. A higher degree of innovativeness is expected to contribute to the early adoption of the innovation. Diffusion takes place in a *social system*. Factors embedded in the social system include the presence and engagement of local opinion builders, the preparedness of leaders to encourage and support adoption, and the adopter's perception of the push for adoption. The necessary stages of the *individual adoption process* includes awareness of an innovation, understanding the value and merit of the innovation, motivation and decision to adopt the innovation, implementation of the innovation, and, finally, securing sustainability of the adoption. A target-oriented diffusion system includes a change agency with trained change promoters who approach and work with opinion leaders within a social system.

The Evidence-Based Practice Movement

Greater awareness of the need for ethical, high-quality, safe, and transparent services among service users and policy makers led to the emergence of the movement that became known as evidence-based medicine (EBM), later referred to as EBP and evidence-based social work practice (EBSWP). Ideas about EBM began to emerge prior to the establishment of the Cochrane Collaboration in 1993. Most notably, David Sackett and Brian Haynes at McMaster University in Canada coined the term "evidence-based medicine" in reference to a process of integrating current best available scientific evidence with patient preferences and clinical experience. The term entered the curriculum in medical schools. Sackett and his colleagues first published their now classic book *Evidence-based Medicine: How to Practice and Teach EBM* in 1997.

Seen in a historical perspective, EBP and evidence-based policy making were developed as an approach to deal with the uncertainty of whether an efficient intervention would work in real-life situations. In this sense, EBP has a mission very similar to what is being developed as translational research and implementation. Well-conducted and robust RCTs and well-performed meta-analyses of a select group of high-quality effectiveness studies provide good estimates of whether an intervention works or is harmful. The important question, though, that practitioners and decision makers have to consider is whether an intervention works in individual cases under specific conditions. Or, will an intervention work in a social context for which it was not tested? This is the limitation of any high-quality evidence on the effectiveness of interventions. EBP is the integration of scientific evidence, clinical skills, and client preferences for sound decision-making in the care of clients. Thus, there is a natural complementarity between the Cochrane and Campbell collaborations and the EBP process. However, because practitioners and decision makers have to deal with a broad range of real-life problems and the Cochrane and Campbell collaborations are limited in their coverage of existing problem areas, the collaborations remain just one type of knowledge source for EBP. Other sources include the primary research community, other systematic review producers, clearinghouses, and other institutions. In comparison to several other suppliers of scientific evidence on effective interventions, the most outstanding merit of the collaborations is the setting of high standards and promotion of scientific transparency in the production of systematic reviews.

The Institutional Context of Translational Research

Components of Research Translation

Before describing the intended nature of translational research, it is necessary to briefly review four related terms: effectiveness, diffusion, dissemination, and implementation. All of these terms have been in use for a number of years and aim to capture various aspects of research translation—that is, enabling innovations to reach the end users for utilization. They provide a backdrop to translational research.

Effectiveness refers to the determination of whether a program or practice works as intended (i.e., does more good than harm) when used in real-world settings. Effectiveness studies differ from efficacy studies in that the latter are conducted under ideal or optimum conditions and are designed to eliminate potentially important confounders (Flay, 1986). The objective of efficacy studies is to create the evidence base that ultimately is translated into practice. However, because optimal conditions are often artificial in the sense that they rarely correspond in their entirety to real-world practice, effectiveness studies are an important step in the translation process.

Lomas (1993) characterizes *diffusion* as a passive and unplanned process that lacks targeted receivers. Diffused information reaches or is captured only by active information seekers who are highly motivated to access the targeted information. Typically, what is being diffused are scientific journal articles, and it is less likely that busy physicians and other end users in general find time to search, retrieve, appraise, and read primary sources such as journal articles.

Dissemination is an intentional process in which the information is tailored and adapted to the needs of the targeted group and then actively communicated to them. Typically, systematic research reviews, practice guidelines, and consensus statements—which in themselves are tools of syntheses and dissemination of large amounts of knowledge—are disseminated rather than diffused to well-defined and targeted groups. Lomas holds that dissemination is an effective form of communication when the purpose is to generate awareness, the information receivers are well defined, and the message is tailored to the needs of the receiver group.

Implementation goes beyond dissemination and involves making an intervention work by identifying and facilitating mechanisms that promote the use of an intervention. However, the boundaries of the implementation process have often been muddled by the existence of several competing definitions. Klein and Sorra (1996), for instance, describe *implementation* as the gateway or phase of innovation that lies between the decision to adopt the innovation and the routine use of the innovation. Fixsen and colleagues (Fixsen, Naoom, Blase, Friedman, & Wallace, 2005) and Aarons and colleagues (Aarons, Hurlburt, & Horwitz, 2011) include a phase of exploration that precedes the decision to adopt as part of the implementation process. Nevertheless, there is growing consensus that implementation is an *active* process of moving science to service (Fixsen, Blase, Naoom, & Wallace, 2009).

"The public policy decisions of governments," writes Lomas, "are diffused through technical, legislative and regulatory statutes available to the knowledgeable and motivated interests. Dissemination of public policy relies, however, on the media and targeted information campaigns originating with government to communicate the intent and practical implications of a legislative statute. Implementation of these same decisions is dependent on a complex framework of sanctions and incentives, reinforced by monitoring and adjustment, and often adapted to fit differing environments at more local levels" (1993, p. 227). The process of getting information on medical or social work innovations would follow a similar path.

The National Institutes of Health

The concept of "translational research" was launched by the National Institutes of Health, the major U.S. federal research foundation that funds research in health, mental health, and related human services areas. To bridge the gap between research and the use of medical evidence, NIH launched a major program in 2004 that came to be known as the *NIH Roadmap for Medical Research*. The Roadmap was originally designed to address specific deficits or gaps in biomedical research. Topics targeted by NIH included fostering high-risk/high-reward research, enabling the development of transformative tools and methodologies, filling fundamental knowledge gaps, and changing academic culture to foster collaboration (http://commonfund.nih.gov).

The *Translational Research Program,* one of the subprograms included in the Roadmap, was designed to reshape the clinical research culture. The main purpose of bringing evidence-based interventions to clinical practice as quickly and efficiently as possible was to bridge basic research and human clinical research. Dr. Elias A. Zerhouni, who served as director of the NIH from 2002 to 2008, wrote:

> Exciting basic science discoveries demand that clinical research continue and even expand, while striving to improve efficiency and better inform basic science.... Clinical research needs to develop new partnerships among organized patient communities, community-based physicians, and academic researchers. In the past, all research for a clinical trial could be conducted in one academic center; that is unlikely to be true in the future. In these initiatives, NIH will promote creation of better integrated networks of academic centers that work jointly on clinical trials and include community-based physicians who care for large groups of well-characterized patients. Implementing this vision will require new ways to organize how clinical research information is recorded, new standards for clinical research protocols, modern information technology, new models of cooperation between NIH

and patient advocacy alliances, and new strategies to reenergize the clinical research workforce (2003, p. 64).

A considerable portion of NIH-funded translational research is now conducted within the framework of the Clinical and Translational Science Awards (CTSA) Consortium launched in October 2006. The consortium began with 12 academic health centers across the United States and was expanded to include an additional 12 centers by September 2007. It is projected that when the consortium reaches full scale, about 60 CTSA centers will be in place. The goal of CTSA is to "1) captivate, advance, and nurture a cadre of well-trained multi- and inter-disciplinary investigators and research teams; 2) create an incubator for innovative research tools and information technologies; and 3) synergize multi-disciplinary and inter-disciplinary clinical and translational research and researchers to catalyze the application of new knowledge and techniques to clinical practice at the front lines of patient care" (http://commonfund. nih.gov/ctsa/overview.aspx).

These centers bring together researchers from various academic fields such as social marketing, behavioral change, organizational change, social anthropology, finance and economics, and medicine. The idea of translational research has also found its way to social work, which is seen as a leading practice and discipline in the delivery of human services.

The Centers for Disease Control and Prevention and the Interactive Systems Framework for Dissemination and Implementation

The CDC is the lead federal agency in the United States for the prevention and control of chronic and infectious diseases, injuries, workplace hazards, disabilities, and environmental and occupational health threats. This vital and comprehensive role in a country of more than 300 million people necessitates the use of the most effective means of informing and educating individuals, organizations, and populations. CDC is constantly searching for and developing effective systems to disseminate and implement evidence-based interventions and innovations.

A CDC Division of Violence Prevention research team recently developed the Interactive Systems Framework for Dissemination and Implementation (ISF) to compensate for some of the shortcomings of previous models of innovation dissemination and implementation, including source-based models in which innovation is transferred from the innovation developer (source) to user (including Rogers' diffusion of innovation theory) and user-based models in which user awareness of a need for innovation is the driving factor (Wandersman et al., 2008). A limitation of earlier linear models like the Institute of Medicine's (Mrazek & Haggerty, 1994) innovation diffusion model for prevention is that they focus on functions of the dissemination and implementation process (such as introduction, selection, and adoption of the innovation) and fall short of examining the infrastructure that facilitates these functions. The ISF is designed to supplement the final steps of the IOM model—serving as a bridge between large-scale trials of an intervention and ultimate implementation and evaluation of an intervention in a community setting.

The ISF integrates three systems or sets of activities: the Prevention Synthesis and Translation System, the Prevention Support System, and the Prevention Delivery System.

The activities of the Prevention Synthesis and Translation System are focused on information retrieval, synthesis, and translation of evidence-based innovation information into plain language and user-friendly forms. As described earlier in this chapter, these types of tasks are also performed by other networks, such as the Cochrane and Campbell collaborations and various evidence-based clearinghouses. The Prevention Support System operates through two mechanisms: general capacity building and innovation-specific capacity building. General capacity-building activities include enhancement of the infrastructure, motivation, and readiness of an organization that will adopt an innovation. Innovation-specific capacity building refers to providing information about the innovation before an adoption decision is made, training in how the innovation should be implemented, and technical assistance once the innovation is implemented. The Prevention Delivery System operates through the mechanisms of general capacity use and innovation-specific capacity use. The former facilitates the functioning of an organization by making sure that there is supportive leadership in place, the adoption motivation is maintained, there is an adequate number of staff available, etc. Innovation-specific capacity use refers to the maintenance of all elements of an innovation to secure the implementation process. The ISF model is described as a heuristic by its developers (Wandersman et al., 2008). The model (Figure 2.1) is constructed to function in a context of factors that include macro policy issues, funding, available research on innovations, and cultural climate in terms of openness to adoption of innovations.

At the current stage, ISF is a theoretical model and has not been tested in real-life situations. Its merit and value in real-life situations of translational efforts need to be verified empirically.

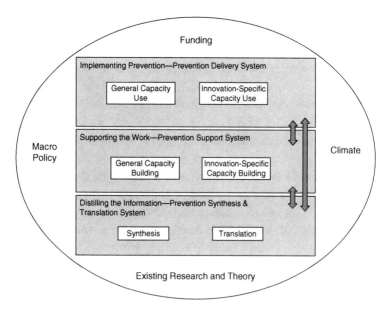

FIGURE 2.1 *ISF Model*

(*Source:* Wandersman et al., 2008, p. 174.)

From Evidence to Utilization

This section describes the path of evidence production that came to be known as Type I, II, and III research. Traditionally, natural and social scientists used the terms *basic research* and *applied research* to distinguish between research conducted without and with practical application purposes, respectively. Differentiation of scientific activities created a gap between knowledge generation and application. Efforts to develop a science of translation have aimed to bridge this gap. The Roadmap designed by the U.S. NIH illustrates this point.

The original NIH Roadmap was designed for biomedical research to capture three stages of the process from basic research to implementation—basic science research (bench), human clinical research (bedside), and utilization of results in clinical practice. Basic science research includes preclinical and animal-based studies that may or may not lead to any useful results for human clinical application. Human clinical research is the implementation and study of basic research outcomes in human clinical conditions. These studies are conducted in controlled settings and thus do not integrate everyday (uncontrolled or uncontrollable) variations of treatment settings. Useful results of clinical research are usually refined in systematic research reviews and meta-analyses such as those generated by the Cochrane Collaboration, in practice guidelines, and in recommendations processed by national agencies. In the Roadmap, the translation between bench and bedside is known as "T1," and the translation between bedside and clinical practice is known as "T2."

However, not much of these research results reach patients in ambulatory settings (USDHHS, 2009; IOM, 2001; PNFCMH, 2003). Westfall and colleagues (Westfall, Mold, & Fagnan, 2007) propose that an additional stage, practice-based research—defined as research on the effectiveness and sustainability of recommended social work treatments in real social work agency environment applications—be added to the chain between basic research and ultimate patient treatment. This stage would involve clinical trials, observational studies, and surveys but also the development of guidelines, meta-analyses, systematic reviews, and dissemination and implementation research.

Practice-based research involves observational studies in real-life conditions. In fact, this proposition is not unknown to biomedical and social research. What Westfall and colleagues are proposing is traditionally known as *effectiveness research*, the study of efficient treatments or interventions in real-life conditions. Nevertheless, their proposal is instrumental and helps to clarify a deficit of the NIH Roadmap conceptualization. The third translational stage, T3, refers to moving new medical treatments and innovations into day-to-day medical practice. T3 is supported by dissemination and implementation research. We agree with Westfall and his colleagues that:

> Well positioned to conduct translational research, practice-based research is not synonymous with translational research. Practice-based research may be the best setting for studying the process of care and the manner in which diseases are diagnosed, treatments initiated, and chronic conditions managed. It is in practice-based research where effectiveness can be measured, where new clinical questions may arise, where readiness to change and adopt new treatments can be studied and addressed, where patient knowledge and preferences are encountered and managed, and where the interface between patients and their physicians can be explored and medical care improved. Practice-based research is the final common pathway for improving individual patient care and outcomes (2007, p. 406).

Translation and Implementation in Social Work Discipline and Practice

In this context, it is informative to examine the declarations of some of the leading social work professional organizations. For instance, the International Federation of Social Workers (IFSW) prescribes the following:

> The social work profession promotes social change, problem solving in human relationships and the empowerment and liberation of people to enhance well-being. Utilising theories of human behaviour and social systems, social work intervenes at the points where people interact with their environments. Principles of human rights and social justice are fundamental to social work . . . . Social work bases its methodology on a systematic body of evidence-based knowledge derived from research and practice evaluation, including local and indigenous knowledge specific to its context (2000, para. 1).

Similarly, the code of ethics of the National Association of Social Workers (NASW) in the United States prescribes the following: "Social workers should provide services in substantive areas or use intervention techniques or approaches that are new to them only after engaging in appropriate study, training, consultation, and supervision from people who are competent in those interventions or techniques" (2008, section 1.04, para. 2).

In social work, there is a high degree of emphasis on social change, problem solving in human relationships, and the empowerment and liberation of people from hardship to enhance well-being. The principles of human rights and social justice are fundamental to the social work profession. Furthermore, it is a universal imperative that social workers use high-quality knowledge and skills to determine whether social work interventions work, may cause harm to the client, or, most desirably, are effective in the betterment of the client's situation (Soydan, 2008).

Interventions for the betterment of clients—whether individuals, groups, or communities—constitute the core of social work practice. Consequently, diffusion, dissemination, and implementation of evidence-based interventions are the vehicles to fulfill the core practical and ethical mission of the social work profession—namely, improvement of the human condition.

Additional Resources

For additional information on research designs:

Shadish, W. R., Cook, T. D., & Campbell, D. T. (2002). *Experimental and quasi-experimental designs for generalized causal inference.* Boston, MA: Houghton Mifflin.

For additional information on the use of evidence-based practices:

Carden, F. (2009). *Knowledge to policy: Making the most of development research.* New Delhi, India: Sage.

Nutley, S. M., Walter, I., & Davies, H. T. O. (2007). *Using evidence: How research can inform public services.* Bristol, England: Policy Press.

For additional information on evidence-based clearinghouses:

Soydan, H., Mullen, E. J., Alexandra, L., Rehnman, J., & Li, Y.-P. (2010). Evidence-based clearinghouses in social work. *Research on Social Work Practice, 20*(6), 690–700. doi: 10.1177/1049731510367436

3

Research on Translation and Implementation

The purpose of this chapter is to explore the efforts by social work professionals to translate and implement evidence-based interventions. After having discussed the context of translation and implementation of evidence-based practices in the previous chapter, here we focus on what the social work profession may teach us in terms of understanding translation and implementation in social work contexts.

Multisystemic Therapy

Multisystemic Therapy (MST) (Schoenwald, 2009) is a family- and community-based treatment developed for delinquent youth at risk of incarceration or other restrictive out-of-home treatment settings. It is widely used in the treatment of chronic, violent, and substance-abusing juvenile delinquents. Consistent with Bronfenbrenner's (1979) theory of social ecology, MST works with youth in family, peer, school, neighborhood, and community settings. Typically, MST is provided for 3 to 5 months by clinicians who are organized into small teams (two to four professionals) and a supervisor. Each team usually has a caseload of four to six families at a time. The duration and frequency of the treatment provided vary with the circumstances of the family. MST interventions focus on treating a number of dysfunctions using treatment techniques that have the most empirical support. MST interventions aim at improving caregiver discipline and monitoring practices, reducing family conflict, improving affective relations, reducing youth interaction with deviant peers, promoting interaction with prosocial peers, and improving academic and vocational performance. Furthermore, the interventions focus on developing an indigenous network of family members, friends, and neighbors to support the treatment process and the family's ability to sustain treatment outcomes in the long term.

MST is an intervention program supported by a well-developed organizational infrastructure, MST Services (http://www.mstservices.com), a Limited Liability Corporation (LLC) for-profit organization that markets and manages the intervention model. A number of issues may limit the implementation of MST; difficulties are mainly cost related and include purchase of implementation rights, training and consultation, and monitoring. MST program development at any given site is a process initiated by a community request to MST Services. It might take up to a year to establish an MST program in a community. Initial preparations are processed in several steps.

- Initial information collection helps assess the feasibility of the MST program at a particular site. The MST needs assessment procedure is designed to determine whether the needs of a community can be met by MST; the assessment is expected to identify a clearly defined target population, funding sustainability to keep the program going, and cultivation of commitments from the service agency to implement the MST program with fidelity. At this point, community stakeholders and the MST purveyor make a decision on whether to continue with the program development.
- If the process continues, the next step is to hold "MST critical issues sessions" to identify and discuss issues such as inclusion/exclusion criteria, discharge criteria, and outcomes measurements. A site readiness review meeting is held with professionals who will be responsible for the day-to-day activities of the MST implementation. Follow-up conference calls and other meetings are scheduled as needed to support MST and provider agency goals and organizational procedures.
- A 5-day orientation training then begins before the clients are admitted. After the program starts, ongoing training and

support are provided to the MST staff. This continuing support includes quarterly booster training, weekly on-site supervision, and weekly consultation with an MST expert from MST Services.

A large number of outcome studies were conducted by the program developers and independent evaluators to measure the effectiveness of MST in the United States and elsewhere. Most studies have identified MST as one of the most effective treatment programs for serious antisocial behavior in adolescents at risk of incarceration (Schoenwald, 2009). There have also been failures to successfully replicate MST. For example, a recent multisite trial conducted in Sweden has failed to find outcomes favoring the MST condition (Sundell et al., 2008). An earlier, unpublished trial in Ontario, Canada (Leschied & Cunningham, 2002) found reductions in conviction rates well below those found in published trials of MST. However, the quantity and quality of the adherence data collected in each site are mostly unknown, and it is known that overall adherence was lowest in the site with the most negative outcomes. Perhaps the most controversial publication that challenged MST's effectiveness is a Campbell Collaboration systematic review including a meta-analysis of MST effectiveness studies by Littell, Campbell, Green, and Toews (2005). This review concluded that MST was not significantly more effective than alternative services in reducing juvenile delinquency and out-of-home placements. However, this review remains contested (Ogden & Hagen, 2006).

Thus far, dissemination and transport of MST have been intensive and expansive in the United States and a number of other countries. One of the developers of MST, Sonja Schoenwald, characterizes the diffusion of MST as an S-curve similar to the one observed by Everett Rogers in the diffusion and adoption of agricultural technology innovations (Schoenwald, 2010). Initial demand for MST transport on a larger scale emanated from the South Carolina Department of Juvenile Justice and Department of Mental Health. These agencies supported earlier trials of MST and consequently were informed about the positive results during early development of the intervention. Thus, these South Carolina agencies agreed to a statewide implementation of MST. Concurrently, presentations at juvenile justice and mental health conferences generated demand from agencies in other states. During the early years, university-based researchers provided training of MST staff and follow-up support. As the demand for MST implementation quickly increased, MST Services was established in 1996 to serve users of MST on a commercial basis.

Schoenwald (2010) describes two key federal government initiatives as stimulators of an accelerating adoption of MST. These initiatives were backed by the Office of Juvenile Justice and Delinquency Prevention (OJJDP) and the Substance Abuse and Mental Health Services Administration's (SAMHSA) Center for Mental Health Services (CMHS). Various strategies developed by OJJDP included the establishment of Blueprints for Violence Prevention, an evidence-based clearinghouse for the assessment, rating, and dissemination of evidence-based interventions for violence prevention, and seed funding to develop manuals and other tools for the effective implementation of MST and to conduct a pilot study of the viability of MST implementation in nine states. These measures by OJJDP contributed significantly to the upward movement of the S-curve.

In the early 1990s, MST transport was further enhanced by the federal Comprehensive Community Mental Health Services for Children and Their Families Program, which provided grants to states and communities to develop systems of care to advance child- and family-centered and community-based mental health services for youth with severe emotional disturbances. This program was offered to a majority of states, some of which established MST for youth as a result. Both practice and research generated knowledge about the effectiveness of these adaptations as well as the transfer of training and clinical support from adaptation developers to community-based professionals. Eventually, evidence associated with adaptations of MST for different populations was deposited in the National Registry of Evidence-based Programs and Practices, sponsored by SAMHSA (http://www.nrepp.samhsa.gov).

During the late 1900s and early 2000s, a number of states imported and diffused MST but applied different policies and strategies in the process. State policies are characterized by a continuum from centralized to decentralized mandates (Schoenwald, 2010).

The state of Connecticut adopted a centralized approach; currently, the Department of Children and Families and the Court Support Services Division support the statewide expansion of MST by jointly funding a private provider agency to provide training and support to all MST programs in the state. Contracted providers are directly reimbursed by the state agencies for MST services provided to youth and their families.

In contrast, the implementation of MST in Colorado is completely decentralized and not funded by the state. Initially, MST was introduced to Colorado with federal funding and Blueprints dissemination programs. Currently, the MST network partner in Colorado, the Center for Effective Interventions, supports the majority of the MST programs throughout the state and receives no public funding for its services.

Ohio exemplifies a state situated in the middle of the continuum. The governor's office in Ohio pursued adoption of MST as an initiative to improve services for juvenile offenders. The dissemination of MST was accelerated through the establishment of the Coordinating Centers of Excellence in 1999 across state departments of health, mental health, education, welfare, and juvenile justice. In 2003, the Department of Mental Health established the Center for Innovative Practices (CIP) to support MST programs in Ohio. However, CIP is maintained by payments from provider agencies, funded by local mental health boards.

MST is becoming a global intervention. International transport of MST is also taking different shapes (Schoenwald, 2010). MST was tested nationwide in Norway, where it was introduced and disseminated in a highly centralized fashion. In the Netherlands, as in Colorado, the adoption of MST is organized by private agencies, while in Denmark, as in Ohio, officials chose the middle ground.

Although MST is not exclusively a social work intervention and is implemented by professionals with different educational and organizational backgrounds, it is as much a social work intervention as it is an intervention to support youth with criminal and violent behavior and their families. Typically, MST targets core client groups of the social work profession, including maltreated and neglected children and youth, and adolescents with psychiatric, substance abuse, or sexual behavior problems. Social workers often play a lead role in delivery of MST interventions in social work agency environments. The journey of MST is a good illustration of what it takes to develop and test an innovation and to diffuse and disseminate it, first, nationally and, later, internationally. Not all evidence-based interventions have the benefit of systematic and sustainable support for wider dissemination and implementation. A later section of this chapter offers a number of models of dissemination and implementation of social work interventions. Next, however, is an overview of factors associated with diffusion, dissemination, and implementation of innovations in health service delivery organizations based on an extensive literature review conducted by Greenhalgh, Robert, Macfarlane, Bate, and Kyriakidou (2004).

Models of Translation and Implementation Process

Barriers and Facilitators of Evidence-Based Practice Translation

The literature review by Greenhalgh and colleagues (2004, p. 582) is a synthesis of 495 sources, including 213 empirical and 282 nonempirical studies. These contributions represent a large number of research traditions such as rural sociology, medical sociology, communication studies, marketing, development studies, health promotion, evidence-based medicine, organizational studies, knowledge utilization, narrative studies, and complexity studies. Based on this review, the authors introduce a conceptual model for considering the determinants of diffusion, dissemination, and implementation of innovations in health service delivery and organization. It is one of several conceptual models of research translation that have been proposed over the years (Damanpour, 1991; Fixsen et al., 2005; Frambach & Schillewaert, 2002; Klein & Sorra, 1996; Real & Poole, 2005; Rosenheck, 2001; Schoenwald, Kelleher, Weisz, & the Research Network on Youth Mental Health, 2008; Shortell et al., 2001; Simpson, 2002). Although it excludes assessment of effectiveness as outlined in Chapter 1, it is introduced here because it is one of the most comprehensive models published.

Greenhalgh and colleagues distinguish among "*diffusion* (passive spread), *dissemination* (active and planned efforts to persuade target groups to adopt an innovation), *implementation* (active and planned efforts to mainstream an innovation within an organization), and *sustainability* (making an innovation routine until it reaches obsolescence)" (2004, p. 582). Diffusion and dissemination of innovations are influenced by the characteristics of the innovation and the outer context that, in itself, embraces a number of crucial factors such as an individual's propensity to accept innovations, organizational readiness for innovations, and interaction between various organizations.

Characteristics of the Innovation

The following characteristics of the innovation synthesized by the Greenhalgh et al. review may affect innovation diffusion as facilitators or inhibiters. On the basis of these characteristics, recommendations can be made to promote innovation diffusion, dissemination, and implementation.

- *Relative advantage.* To adopt innovations, potential users look for the relative advantages of an innovation in terms of effectiveness or cost-effectiveness. Often, potential users study and negotiate the innovations, including evidence-based interventions.
- *Compatibility.* Potential users look for interventions that are compatible with their values, norms, and perceived needs. Organizations tend to adopt innovations that are consistent with their values, norms, and culture.

- *Complexity*. Innovations that are simple are adopted more often than are innovations with a high degree of complexity.
- *Trialability*. Innovations are more likely to be adopted if the potential users can experiment with and test the innovation to learn more about it.
- *Observability*. Potential users of innovations are more likely to adopt if the benefits of the innovation are visible.
- *Reinvention*. If potential users can modify and adapt innovations to suit their perceived needs, an innovation will be more likely to be adopted.
- *Fuzzy boundaries*. Complex innovations tend to have a core of irreducible elements and a set of peripheral elements associated with organizational and systemic structures. If peripheral elements can be modified and adapted, an innovation is more likely to be adopted.
- *Risk*. Introduction of an innovation is associated with risk and uncertainty. A higher degree of perceived risk decreases the likelihood of adoption.
- *Task relevance*. If an intervention is pertinent to the task of the potential user, it will be adopted more easily.
- *Knowledge required to use an innovation*. If the knowledge required to adopt an innovation can be transferred from one context to another (transportability), the innovation will be more likely to be adopted.

Absorption and Assimilation of Innovations by Organizations

Due to its historical development, professional social work practice typically takes place within organizations, whether they are small or large, public or private, and specialized or comprehensive. Therefore, when it comes to social work and other human service professions, adoption of innovations or innovative interventions becomes a matter of an organization's willingness, readiness, and ability to adopt an innovation and to make sure that it is accepted and implemented by individual workers. In organizational settings, adoption of innovations involves various levels of the organization, innovation awareness, innovation selection, adoption, and implementation. System readiness is a crucial factor for the adoption, implementation, and maintenance of an innovation.

The following elements of system readiness were identified by Greenhalgh et al. (2004):

- *Tension for change.* The organization is more likely to successfully adopt an innovation if its staff perceives the current conditions in the organization as intolerable.
- *Innovation–system fit.* When an innovation is compatible with the values, norms, strategies, goals, skills, and technologies of an organization, the organization will have a higher degree of readiness for the introduction of an innovation.
- *Assessment of implications.* If the implications of the innovation are fully assessed and known within the organization, there will be a higher degree of readiness for adoption.

Furthermore, if supporters of the innovation outnumber its opponents, the allocation of resources is adequate, and the ability to evaluate the innovation is present, the likelihood that the organization will adopt an innovation will be greater.

Interorganizational Context of Innovation Diffusion

Greenhalgh et al. (2004) found that a number of interorganizational factors may promote or inhibit the decision by an organization's managers to adopt an innovation.

- *Organizational networks.* When a sufficient proportion of comparable organizations adopt an innovation, other organizations tend to follow suit. Thus, organizations that are well connected to other comparable organizations in networks are more susceptible to the network impact in terms of adopting innovations.
- *Intentional spread strategies.* There is some evidence suggesting that formal, intentional initiatives to "scale up" innovations

among a network of organizations (e.g., social work agencies run by counties) may work at times. However, such initiatives tend to be expensive, resulting in limited cost-effectiveness.

- *Wider environment.* Although common wisdom suggests that environmental factors impact the adoption of innovations by organizations, the review found very limited evidence to support this proposition. Research on these factors was diffuse such that different aspects of the "environment" were examined without a sufficient accumulation of evidence to confirm any specific role of the environment.
- *Political directives.* Especially when associated with funding support, political directives may increase successful adoption and implementation of innovations in organizations.

Routinization and Sustainability of Innovations

A decision to adopt an innovation extends to and becomes intertwined with the implementation phase of an innovation; any implemented innovation must be secured by factors to support routinization and sustainability of the innovation within the organization. Lack of routinization and sustainability will cause failure of the innovation.

- *Organizational structure.* Organizations that are adaptive and flexible will be able to support and enhance routinization of an innovation and will provide sustainable and continuing implementation.
- *Leadership of the organization.* Innovations will be increasingly routinized and become sustainable if the leadership of the organization is supportive and enhances the implementation process, and later provides a continuing funding stream. Sustainability is further enhanced if the innovation aligns with the existing goals of the top and middle managers of the organization.
- *Human resources.* Organizations that are populated with practitioners who are motivated and have the skills and capacity to

maintain successful implementation of an innovation will more often establish and sustain the innovation.

- *Funding.* There is strong direct evidence that dedicated and continued funding has a strong positive impact on the routinization of an innovation in human services organizations.
- *Intraorganizational communication.* The reviewers found strong indirect evidence that organizations with good intradepartmental communication, especially if they generate positive narratives to support the implementation of the innovation, more often routinize innovations.
- *Interorganizational networks.* The role of interorganizational support becomes more important when the implementation of an innovation is more complex.
- *Feedback.* The chance of successful routinization is increased by timely and accurate information transfer within the organization. As mentioned earlier, efficient data collection and review systems need to be developed to generate accurate and timely information on the adoption and implementation processes.
- *Adaptation.* Routinization is more likely when, if needed, an innovation is adapted to local circumstances.

Diffusion, dissemination, implementation, and retention of evidence-based interventions involve complex processes that may be unique each time an intervention is adopted by a service organization. The main trajectory of the translation of MST may or may not be the same for other interventions adopted in service organizations. Experience from hundreds of other cases can be distilled to understand factors that facilitate (or inhibit) effective adoption of interventions, as evidenced by the Greenhalgh et al. review. Factors that stand out as facilitators and inhibitors are an empirical issue to be studied in each individual case. Social work organizations may or may not behave like health care delivery organizations; how they behave is an empirical issue as well. Nevertheless, a typology of important factors that affect adoptions is useful in developing and refining evidence-based interventions in organizations for various types of service delivery.

Implementation Stages and Core Components

In 2005, Fixsen and colleagues published a major review and synthesis of literature on implementation research. In this review, the authors distilled various dimensions of implementation science and designed a roadmap for future development. This work later become a backdrop to the development of the National Implementation Research Network (NIRN) (http://www.fpg.unc.edu/~nirn) and then the Global Implementation Conference (http://www.implementationconference.org).

This review identified six stages of implementation:

- *Exploration and adoption.* The purpose of exploration is to assess the potential match between community needs, evidence-based program needs, and community resources and then to make a decision regarding whether to proceed. At the end of the exploration stage, a decision is made to proceed with implementation of an evidence-based program in a given community or state based on formal and informal criteria developed by the community and with use of the evidence-based program.
- *Installation.* This stage is focused on the development of structural supports necessary to initiate the program, including ensuring the availability of funding streams, human resources strategies, and policy development, as well as creating referral mechanisms, reporting frameworks, and outcome expectations. Additional resources may be needed to realign current staff, hire new staff members to meet the qualifications required by the program or practice, secure appropriate space, purchase needed technology (e.g., cell phones, computers), fund un-reimbursed time in meetings with stakeholders, and fund time for staff while they are in training.
- *Initial implementation.* This stage is characterized by changes in skill levels, organizational capacity, and organizational culture. These changes may be more or less dramatic for an individual or organization. The ability of either to adapt or accommodate

to these changes will determine whether the implementation process effectively ends at this point or proceeds to subsequent stages.

- *Full operation.* Once the new learning becomes integrated into practitioner, organizational, and community practices, policies, and procedures, the implemented program becomes fully operational with full staffing complements and full client loads. At this point, the innovation becomes standard practice and "treatment as usual."

- *Innovation.* Efforts to implement new evidence-based practices in new settings present opportunities to refine and expand both the treatment practices and programs and the implementation practices and programs. These activities potentially lead to improvement in service delivery and potentially additional experimental studies to confirm their effectiveness.

- *Sustainability.* The goal during this stage is the long-term survival and continued effectiveness of the implementation despite changes in staffing, leadership, funding streams, program requirements, and external demands and supports.

Based on the commonalities among successful implementation programs, Fixsen and colleagues (2009) identified seven core components:

- *Staff selection.* This involves the identification and recruitment of current or new staff possessing both the skills and motivation necessary to learn and apply innovative practices.

- *Preservice and in-service training.* These activities provide new knowledge and values, components and rationales of key practices, and opportunities to learn new practice skills and receive feedback.

- *Overall coaching and consultation.* "A coach provides 'craft' information along with advice, encouragement, and opportunities to practice and use skills specific to the innovation (e.g., engagement, treatment planning, clinical judgment" (p. 534).

- *Staff performance assessment.* This "is designed to assess the use and outcomes of skills that are reflected in the selection criteria, taught in training, and reinforced and expanded in coaching processes" (p. 534).
- *Decision support data systems.* This involves the systematic collection of data on quality improvement, organizational fidelity, and consumer outcomes that are used to support decision making.
- *Facilitative administration.* These administrators provide leadership and rely on a range of data sources to inform decision making, support the overall processes, and keep staff focused on the desired EBP outcomes.
- *Systems interventions.* These are strategies to ensure the availability of financial, organizational, and human resources required to support the work of the practitioners.

The following section offers a number of models that are being tested, with special reference to social work and other human service organizations that are important support systems for social work.

Models of Research Translation Strategies

Although the model developed by Greenhalgh and colleagues can help social workers to identify barriers and facilitators to translating research into practice, they do not offer specific suggestions for how to facilitate the process of translation. In the field of health services, there exist numerous models that are themselves evidence-based strategies for translation of evidence-based programs, practices, and interventions. In this section, we review some of models of translation strategy that have potential relevance for social work practice. Other strategies include the Institute for Healthcare Improvement (2004) Breakthrough Series (BTS), the Department of Veterans Affairs Health Services Research and Development Service's Quality Enhancement Research Initiative (QUERI) model

(Demakis, McQueen, Kizer, & Feussner, 2000), the Cascading Implementation Model (Chamberlain, Price, Reid, & Landsverk, 2008), and the Community Development Team Model (Sosna & Marsenich, 2006).

RE-AIM Model

The RE-AIM model, developed by Russell E. Glasgow and his colleagues (http://www.re-aim.org), is often used to understand and monitor the feasibility and success of intervention effectiveness, dissemination, and implementation in real-life settings. The acronym RE-AIM stands for Reach, Efficacy/Effectiveness, Adoption, Implementation, and Maintenance. Originally, RE-AIM was developed out of the needs observed in health care delivery service organizations, but because the model has been empirically tested in various local contexts, it has evolved as a model of translation and implementation of innovations in diverse settings of service delivery, including social work (Glasgow, 2009).

Reach pertains to the absolute number, proportion, and representativeness of individuals who are willing to participate in an intervention. Information about representativeness is vital because if those participating are not representative of those eligible for the intervention, the potential of the intervention to be successful in real-life settings becomes uncertain. Reach also emphasizes availability of information on the characteristics of the setting (organization, agency, and culture) where the intervention is implemented, as well as the staff who deliver the intervention.

Efficacy/Effectiveness refers to intended and negative outcomes, as well as effects on quality of life and economic impact. The E/E factor is measured at the participant level and aims to determine outcomes of the intervention, conducted either in compliance with predetermined guidelines under highly controlled conditions or in real-world situations.

Adoption addresses the question of where and for whom this program works and under what specific conditions. Characteristics of the intervention setting and the staff who deliver the intervention, presence of specific mediators, and other contextual factors are essential to understanding success. As experienced by reviewers with the Cochrane and Campbell collaborations, who routinely seek information pertinent to adoption in published and unpublished studies of interventions, researchers seldom report such important information. Knowing the absolute number, proportion, and representativeness of settings and change agents is crucial.

Implementation refers to both individual and organizational levels and pertains to the individual client's use of intervention strategies, as well as the intervention agents' program fidelity, including the intervention protocol, delivery consistency across program components, staff, overtime, duration, and costs.

Maintenance refers to both individual and organizational levels as well. On the individual level, the long-term effectiveness of an intervention is usually measured 6 months or more after the most recent intervention input. Yet most, but not all, interventions require long-term maintenance; some interventions are designed for short-term impact. On the organizational level, researchers are expected to observe whether a successful intervention is institutionalized so as to become a routine practice. Unfortunately, maintenance studies conducted at the organizational level are not very common.

RE-AIM has been applied in a large number of studies to explore various dimensions prescribed by the model's framework. Although most of these studies are primarily associated with health and mental health issues, RE-AIM is a good candidate to use to trace the success of social work interventions (Glasgow, 2009). Figure 3.1 illustrates the RE-AIM model and displays the questions a social worker typically should ask in a research translation situation.

Precede-Proceed Model

The Precede-Proceed (P-P) model was developed by Lawrence Green and Marshall Kreuter, both public health researchers and practitioners. The P-P model is extensively described in their seminal book *Health Program Planning: An Educational and Ecological Approach*,

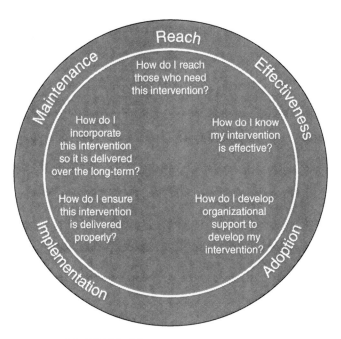

FIGURE 3.1 *RE-AIM Model*

first published in 1980 and currently available in its fourth edition (Green & Kreuter, 2005).

The P-P model is designed for diagnostic planning, implementation, and evaluation of population-based health programs. It takes an ecological and educational approach to handling the complexities of human environments and allowing individual agencies to work on and interact with environmental factors. Furthermore, the model is constructed to use flexibility to respect the varied context of public health programs.

The P-P model's ecological approach builds on the insight that quality of life and health and mental status are heavily influenced by and depend on a system of social and environmental factors known as social determinants of health. Examples of such factors include cost of living (associated with obesity), introduction of walking trails and bike paths (associated with increased cardiovascular fitness), and unemployment and poverty rates (associated with chronic diseases, poor mental health, violence, and poor school performance). Green and Kreuter also built an educational dimension into their model on the assumption that education develops awareness, skills, and knowledge to influence behavior and actions, in addition to generating cultural sensitivity, volitional participation, and informed consent to develop programs for health improvement. Furthermore, the model is based on the assumption that population health programs take place in diverse locales such as workplaces, health care facilities, schools, social work agencies, and neighborhoods. Health care planners and interventionists need to handle contextual characteristics with sensitivity. A culturally sensitive approach would likely lead to an increased probability that the target population will identify the intervention with their needs and would generate trust between health workers and the recipients of the intervention.

The acronym Precede stands for Predisposing, Reinforcing, and Enabling Constructs in Educational Diagnosis and Evaluation and aims to support a diagnostic planning process in the development of targeted public health programs. Precede consists of five steps: determine the needs and social problems of a population; identify the health determinants of those problems and needs; analyze the behavioral and environmental determinants of the health problems; identify factors that are predisposed to, reinforce, and enable the behaviors; and identify the interventions that would work best to prevent, block, or eradicate the problems (see Figure 3.2).

Proceed is an acronym for Policy, Regulatory, and Organizational Constructs in Educational and Environmental Development and serves as a guide for the implementation and evaluation of the interventions designed under the Precede process. Proceed includes four steps: implement the interventions identified; evaluate the process of implementation; evaluate the impact of the interventions on the factors supporting the behavior; and evaluate the impact of the interventions with regard to the quality of life of the target population.

Over the years, the P-P model has been applied in many fields such as public health, community health, and population health

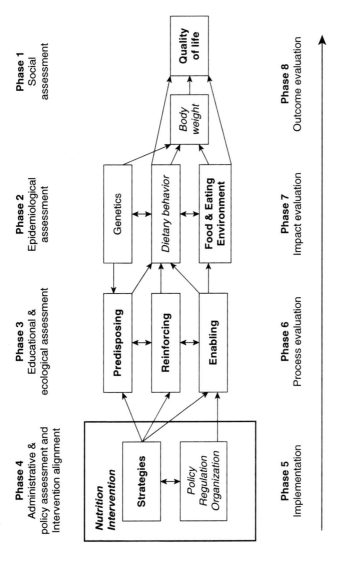

FIGURE 3.2 *Precede-Proceed Model*

(*Source:* Green & Kreuter, 2005, p. 10.)

planning and in the evaluation of diverse settings, including schools, workplaces, health care settings, and neighborhoods. Green and Kreuter note that they found 950 P-P application studies at the time of publication of their 2005 edition. Several chapters of the book are dedicated to presentations of multiple applications, some of which have a high degree of relevance to social work practice.

Availability, Responsiveness, Continuity Model

The Availability, Responsiveness, Continuity (ARC) model is a community- and organization-oriented model that emphasizes the role of the social context in the implementation of evidence-based interventions (Glisson, 2002; Glisson, Dukes, & Green, 2006; Glisson & Green, 2006; Glisson & Shoenwald, 2005). The core purpose of the model is to deliver an evidence-based treatment effectively and with high quality to clients in a specific social and organizational environment. The model is based on three fundamental assumptions: (1) the implementation of an evidence-based intervention, which is an innovation or core technology, is a social process as much as it is professional and technical; (2) social and mental health services are delivered in a complex context of organizations and social institutions including service providers, services organizations, family, and community; and (3) effectiveness of service delivery is a function of how well the evidence-based intervention is mediated by the social environment in which it is delivered. The context of the ARC model is depicted in Figure 3.3.

Typically, this model builds an implementation strategy by studying, understanding, and operationalizing organizational and interorganizational factors in each given implementation context. Drawing on empirical research on how organizations work, it is assumed that the needs of service providers must be met in discussion and collaboration with them and that they must be engaged in designing implementation strategies. In service provider organizations, organizational culture and climate are important factors that affect an organization's effectiveness and attitudes; performance can be improved through organizational development. When multiple aspects of organizational factors are included in strategy

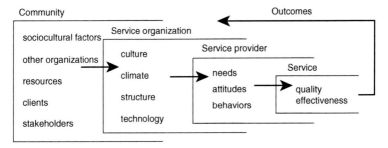

FIGURE 3.3 *Social Context of the ARC Model*

(*Source:* Gilsson & Schoenwald, 2005.)

development, organizational performance increases in the implementation of evidence-based interventions. On an organizational level, the ARC model integrates characteristics of the organizational setting with the evidence-based intervention.

Because service provider organizations operate in a larger social context of other organizations, community stakeholders, and other important local actors, the ARC model aims to integrate the context of the service provider organization with the broader context of interorganizational factors. ARC development strategies focus especially on county government, community and business sectors, and important local opinion leaders such as school principals, judges, and ministers. On the interorganizational level, any given context integrated in the implementation strategy becomes the interorganizational domain.

When developed, the components of the ARC model included a set of activities to drive forward the implementation. These strategies (Glisson, 2002) are listed in the following box.

1. *Participatory decision making* mobilizes all important actors such as service providers and opinion builders to engage with administrative and procedural processes that affect the delivery of the evidence-based intervention.

2. With the assistance of a change agent, *teams are built* to bring together community leaders and service providers who can approach issues together to ease the delivery of the evidence-based intervention.

3. Service teams engage with *continuous quality improvement* using data-based problem analysis to effect change in organizational policies and administrative procedures such as referral procedures and assignment of cases to ease the work of service providers.

4. To eliminate barriers to effective service created by existing job descriptions in a service provider organization, *jobs redesign* efforts are introduced to help providers adapt their ways of working to the requirements of the evidence-based intervention being implemented.

5. A project change agent *develops a network* of service providers, organizational representatives, and community leaders to address concerns of the end users.

6. The change agent provides *feedback* about progress and relapses of the implementation effort to service providers and all other parties involved in the process.

7. The change agent provides *information and assessment strategies* to the community and its representatives to inform and educate about how to use administrative data to assess the implementation process and enforce improvement.

8. Change agents *develop personal relationships* with community leaders to promote communication, information sharing, and problem solving.

9. *Conflict resolution* procedures supported by strong relationships between all parties are used to discuss and solve differences in perspectives or competing interests that may impede implementation.

10. A last strategic component in this list is the *self-regulation and stabilization* of the implementation of the evidence-based intervention. The aim of this component is to make sure that the service provider organization is self-sustaining in terms of information, training, and tools to continue providing the evidence-based interventions once the implementation project is concluded.

Efforts to analyze the use of the ARC model to facilitate implementation of evidence-based interventions are under way. Glisson and colleagues (2010) recently published the results of a randomized controlled trial of MST and the ARC organizational intervention in reducing problem behavior in delinquent youth residing in 14 rural counties in Tennessee, using a 2 × 2 design in which youth were randomized into receiving MST or treatment as usual and counties were randomized into receiving the ARC intervention. A multilevel mixed-effects regression analysis of 6-month treatment outcomes found that total youth problem behavior in the MST plus ARC condition was at a nonclinical level and significantly lower than that in other conditions.

Strategy for Research on Translation and Implementation

This chapter has highlighted several examples of how translation and implementation of evidence-based interventions take place in real-life settings. As an illustrative case, we described the development, dissemination, and implementation of MST; this case study demonstrates the complexity of the process of translating an evidence-based intervention. MST is an early example of diffusion of a social work intervention in which the developers and other parties involved have advanced the worldwide use of MST in a step-by-step manner based on cumulative experiences acquired each time the program was implemented. A complex interplay of organizational, environmental, and intervention characteristics clearly affects the way in which an intervention may be implemented. We also described other models of implementation of evidence-based social work and interventions that have recently been, or are being, tested in real-life contexts. These experimental approaches emphasize different characteristics of the implementation process but also focus on organizational and environmental components that are similar. For instance, while the RE-AIM and P-P models detail various steps of implementation differently, both models carefully investigate the circumstances that may affect implementation. Furthermore, we referred extensively to two systematic literature reviews of studies of innovation diffusion and implementation. These reviews reveal a large number of variables in organizations, environments, and innovations that may affect the diffusion/dissemination and implementation processes.

The closing section of this chapter introduces a strategy for research on translation and implementation of evidence-based interventions. This strategy is based the three activities that are critical to the translation of research evidence into practice: (1) determination of the effectiveness of EBPs in real-world settings; (2) dissemination of effective practices and research evidence to support the use of these practices by a larger audience; and (3) implementation of the effective practices within a setting.

Each activity may have one or more of three foci of translational research: (1) process, (2) outcomes, and (3) context. The focus on process includes studies of *how* a practice or intervention operates, is disseminated, or is implemented. The focus on outcomes includes studies of outcomes associated with the   practice itself or studies associated with efforts to disseminate and implement the practice. The focus on context includes both the outer context—the larger system or environment—and the inner context—the organization, groups, and/or individuals involved in providing the intervention.

Of particular interest in the organizational context is how organizational structures and cultures may facilitate or inhibit successful dissemination and implementation of evidence-based practices, and how this understanding may lead to adaptation of existing strategies or the development of new strategies to facilitate successful dissemination and implementation.

Each of these areas of research focus may be examined using one or more of three types of research design: (1) observational, (2) quasi-experimental, and (3) experimental. Observational designs are used to examine ongoing processes of research translation and to identify barriers and facilitators of practice effectiveness, dissemination, and implementation. Experimental designs are used to evaluate practice effectiveness in real-world settings or strategies for dissemination and implementation. Quasi-experimental designs are used for similar purposes when experimental designs are neither feasible nor desirable.

Finally, each research design may involve one or both of two approaches for collection and analysis of data: (1) mixed methods and (2) community-based participatory research. Mixed-methods analysis was developed over the years as a response, and alternative, to the qualitative-versus-quantitative research controversy. This form consists of a group of research designs in which the researcher combines qualitative and quantitative research designs, data collection methods, analytic approaches, and concepts in a single study. Methods may be combined in various ways, including the use of qualitative and quantitative methods within and across the stages of the research process and integration of a qualitative and a quantitative element in the research process (Tashakkori & Teddlie, 2003). The mixed-methods approach provides great flexibility and support in studies of multifaceted and complex phenomena such as translation and implementation of social work interventions. Mixed methods are addressed further in Chapter 6.

Community-based participatory research (CBPR) emphasizes the participation of members of a community in various aspects of the research process such as problem formulation, data collection, data interpretation, and information dissemination. A partnership between members of the community and professional researchers is assumed to be equal in terms of influencing the research process. By capitalizing on community resources, CBPR aims to generate an understanding of the factors that would support implementation of interventions and yield sustainable results among community members who are affected by the research and implementation (Horowitz, Robinson, & Seifer, 2009). Chapter 7 provides a broad overview of the CBPR approach and its use in social work translational research.

Although translational research typically includes one translational activity (evaluation of effectiveness, dissemination, implementation) and one focus, design, and approach, it may include several different elements from each category in the same research project. Studies of translation and implementation of evidence-based interventions are complex enterprises and require the use of complex research strategies. Hence, a study of evidence-based practice implementation may be embedded in an ongoing effectiveness trial (Brown et al., 2009). A study may have a simultaneous focus on process and context to provide a more comprehensive understanding of EBP, dissemination, and implementation outcomes (Palinkas et al., 2011). A project may sequence observational and experimental/quasi-experimental designs for the sake of adapting an evidence-based practice or a strategy for disseminating or implementing evidence-based practices (Landsverk et al., 2011). Or, mixed methods may be used in combination with a community-based participatory research approach to examine evidence-based practice effectiveness, dissemination, and implementation within the same study.

Choosing from these varied options for conducting translational research should be based on the specific questions to be asked and goals to be accomplished, as well as the available resources and opportunities for conducting such research. Examples of these two criteria will be provided in the next four chapters of this book. In general, it is appropriate for the translational researcher to consider how he or she might answer the following questions. Exactly where in the process of translation is the evidence-based practice that is the focus of the research? Can one understand or influence this process by having one focus, design, and approach, or are combinations of these elements required to achieve the research aims? What resources or opportunities are required to conduct research with a specific focus or foci, design or designs, and approach or approaches? How these questions are answered will dictate the strategy for selecting one or more items from each translational research category to examine one or more activities of research translation.

Additional Resources

For additional information on implementation research:

Greenhalgh, T., Robert, G., Macfarlane, F., Bate, P., & Kyriakidou, O. (2004). Diffusion of innovations in service organizations: Systematic review and recommendations. *Milbank Quarterly*, *82*(4), 581–629.

Manuel, J. I., Mullen, E. J., Fang, L., Bellamy, J. L., & Bledsoe, S. E. (2009). Preparing social work practitioners to use evidence-based practice: A comparison of experience from an implementation project. *Research on Social Work Practice*, *19*(5), 613–627. doi: 10.1177/1049731509335547

Soydan, H. (Guest Ed.). (2009). Implementation and translational research [Special issue]. *Research on Social Work Practice, 19*(5).

4

Research on Process and Outcomes

In this chapter, we review the latest methods in research that focuses on the process and outcomes of research translation in social work practice. Our objective is to argue for the need to examine both process and outcomes simultaneously—i.e., within the same study—because an understanding of one is constrained by a lack of understanding of the other.

Principles and Practice of Research

Evaluating Outcomes, Process, and Context

As noted in Chapter 1, translational research generally has one of three aims: (1) to assess the effectiveness of an evidence-based intervention or practice in a real-world setting in achieving a specific set of outcomes (effectiveness); (2) to assess and contribute to the distribution of information and intervention materials to a specific public health or clinical practice audience (dissemination); and (3) to assess and potentially facilitate or promote its adoption, use, and sustainability in such settings (implementation) (Proctor et al., 2009). The extent to which each of these three aims is accomplished requires an evaluation of outcomes, process, and context. Outcome evaluations focus on determining whether the intervention or practice achieved the intended results. In an effectiveness study, the intended results might be an improvement in health, functioning, or quality of life of individual study participants or groups of participants (e.g., schools, communities). In a dissemination study, the intended result might be the extent to which information is distributed, evaluated, and used by the target audience, which may include practitioners, consumers, or both. In an implementation study, the intended result might be the extent to which a program or practice is adopted, used, and sustained by the target audience, which may range from individual practitioners to organizations to entire systems of care.

Mendel and colleagues distinguish between *outcomes* and *impacts*, the latter defined as "attributable effects of the intervention to wider policy concerns, such as the incidence, prevalence, and social and economic consequences of a particular disease or condition" (Mendel, Meredith, Schoenbaum, Sherbourne, & Wells, 2008, p. 30). Outcomes may also include the degree to which individual clients received evidence-based treatments or services, often referred to as the assessment of the fidelity to which the practice was implemented, and the degree to which the benefits associated with the outcomes exceeded or failed to exceed the costs associated with delivering the program or practice.

However, determinations of whether programs and practices themselves or the strategies for implementing these programs and practices are effective and sustainable in real-world settings cannot be made on the basis of outcomes alone. Outcome evaluation techniques can tell us whether a program or practice works as intended, but it cannot tell us why it worked as it did or give us any insight into the circumstances in which it might not work as intended. Answers to such questions require a focus on the activity itself (process) and the setting or circumstances in which the activity is conducted (context). According to Mendel et al. (2008), without an evaluation of the process in which the program or practice is used, "It is difficult to confidently ascertain *why* certain outcomes were obtained or to explain variation in outcomes in a manner that can be used to improve future intervention design and dissemination strategies..." (p. 30). For instance, researchers or practitioners may intentionally or unintentionally modify or adapt the program or practice during the course of implementation, leading to outcomes deemed to be unsuccessful, successful albeit for unintended reasons, or coincidental. Mendel and colleagues have also "found process evaluations useful in providing 'stories' that illustrate dissemination and implementation processes in ways that are compelling to health services researchers, practitioners, and community members alike" (2008, p. 30). However, process evaluations can be used not merely to facilitate our understanding of variations in outcomes in a summative fashion but also to formatively increase the likelihood that the intended outcomes will be achieved. "Depending on the objectives of a study, it is possible to feed back observations of intervention fidelity, adaptation, and other results of process evaluations to stakeholders during implementation through formative evaluation mechanisms..." (Mendel et al., 2008, p. 30). In doing so, translational research becomes an explicit part of research translation. However, "...evaluators must acknowledge the lack of objectivity inherent in such an approach, even when following rigorous research designs (Bluthenthal et al., 2006), and the timing and effects of such formative feedback must be documented and accounted for as part of the implementation and process evaluation itself" (Mendel et al., 2008, p. 30).

Finally, an understanding of both outcomes and process requires an understanding of the setting or context in which the program or practice is used. According to Mendel et al., "to understand the diffusion of an intervention—why it was or was not adopted, implemented as intended, or sustained over time—and to generalize the feasibility of dissemination and implementation strategies across healthcare and community settings, requires examining the context in which the intervention is introduced" (2008, p. 29). Evaluations of both context and process often provide useful information as to features of the program itself or the setting in which the program is used that may facilitate or impede its successful application, implementation, or sustainability. However, the setting itself may change as new programs are introduced. Employee turnover may increase or the values and behaviors that define the culture and climate of an organization may change. Consequently, "although studies of diffusion commonly measure contextual factors post hoc, it is necessary to conduct prospective 'baseline' assessments of context for initiatives that intend to produce change in the underlying contexts and stakeholder capacities sustaining interventions" (Mendel et al., 2008, p. 29). More will be said about context in the next chapter.

Research Designs

As noted in the previous chapter, empirical translational research usually adopts one of three types of research design: observational, quasi-experimental, or experimental. *Observational designs* have been used to examine barriers and facilitators embedded in the context or associated with the process of disseminating or implementing evidence-based practices . Data are usually collected from a cross section of participants at one point in time or longitudinally during the course of a study. The assessment of agency director perspectives on the challenge of implementing evidence-based practices in community mental health agencies by Proctor and colleagues (Proctor, Knudsen, Fedoravicius, Hovmand, Rosen, & Perron, 2007) is an example of the use of a cross-sectional observational design. In this study, seven executive and clinical directors were interviewed once using a semistructured format. A longitudinal design was used in a series of studies conducted as part of the National Evidence-Based Practice Implementation Project, which explored whether evidence-based practices such as supported employment and integrated dual-disorder treatment could be implemented in routine mental health service settings and identified facilitating conditions, barriers, and strategies that affected implementation (Brunette et al., 2008; Marshall, Rapp, Becker, & Bond, 2008; Marty, Rapp, McHugo, & Whitley, 2008; Rapp et al., 2009; Woltmann et al., 2008). In these studies, data were collected monthly or bimonthly during 2 years by implementation monitors and trainers during site visits, trainings, leadership meetings, and team meetings, by shadowing workers, and through interviews with consumers, direct service workers, supervisors, and workers. Formal fidelity reviews were conducted every 6 months during the implementation and sustaining phase of the project. These data were used to describe changes in fidelity, staff turnover, and implementation processes and outcomes during this 2-year period.

Quasi-experimental designs have been used occasionally in effectiveness studies that evaluate changes in consumer functional status. These studies usually rely on a pre–post design. For instance,

Painter's (2009) study of Multisystemic Therapy (MST) as community-based treatment for youth with severe emotional disturbances used a pretest–posttest quasi-experimental design that had much in common with an overflow design (Rubin & Babbie, 2008). In this design, youth admitted to a community mental health center during a 3-year period were assigned a treatment condition based on whether a slot existed on an MST caseload at the time of assignment and whether the family agreed to services. Youth receiving MST were then compared with youth receiving other services at the same time.

Experimental designs have been used with greater frequency in translational research with the intent of evaluating evidence-based practice effectiveness or specific strategies for disseminating and implementing evidence-based practices. These designs randomize participants either as individuals or as members of groups. Randomization of participants as individuals is widely used in efficacy trials, and in some effectiveness studies where participants are treated individually, treatment groups remain distinct, and an unbiased comparison of an evidence-based practice versus usual care or two evidence-based practices is thus likely (Kramer, 1988). For instance, Ell and colleagues (2009) used this design in a randomized controlled trial (RCT) that compared two interventions: the provision of written resource navigation information (enhanced usual care) versus written information plus patient navigation (TPN) aimed at improving adjuvant treatment adherence and follow-up among 487 low-income, predominantly Hispanic women with breast or gynecological cancer. The TPN model combined interactive health education (decisional support), counseling (emotional support), written care site and community service navigation information, and navigator active assistance to facilitate access and adherence to adjuvant treatment. A Consolidated Standards of Reporting Trials (CONSORT) flowchart detailing study enrollment and attrition over 12 months is given in Figure 4.1.

For some types of effectiveness studies and most types of dissemination and implementation studies, however, individual randomization may actually be detrimental if interaction among

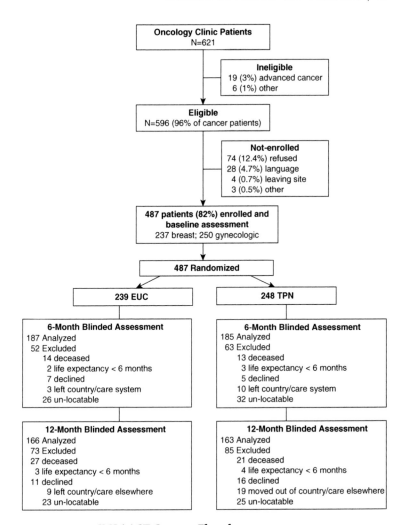

FIGURE 4.1 *IMPAACT Consort Flowchart*

consumers or practitioners may lead to systematic errors in classifying the treatment actually received—that is, the treatments received will be more similar than those allocated, hence a biased comparison (Kramer, 1988, p. 83). Psychosocial, educational, and health service interventions are particularly prone to this problem since subjects are likely to interact with one another between administrations of the intervention and measurement of the outcome. Group randomization is preferable whenever relatively closed and naturally formed groups are capable of modifying the treatment allocated to individuals within these groups (Kramer, 1988). This design is also known as a cluster or blocked design.

Unfortunately, however, group randomization results in a markedly reduced sample size, because the unit of statistical analysis becomes the group, rather than the individual. One alternative, which provides the scientific advantages of group randomization while permitting the statistical advantages of analysis by individual, involves the use of a pretrial study period to demonstrate that individuals in different groups experience similar outcomes when exposed to the same treatment. Equivalent pretrial results increase the plausibility that any differences in outcome that occur when the same groups are exposed to different treatments during the trial are attributed to the treatments, rather than to potentially confounding differences between the groups (Kramer, 1988, p. 84).

Jensen and colleagues (Jensen, Dieterich, Brisson, Bender, & Powell, 2010) evaluated a classroom curriculum aimed at preventing bullying and victimization among elementary students, using a group randomized trial design in which 40 schools were stratified by geographic region and risk criteria and randomly assigned to either the control or the experimental condition. Propensity score matching using a greedy matching method (Guo & Fraser, 2009) was used to redress the imbalance found in the original sample and improve analytical precision.

Data Collection

Outcomes data. With few exceptions, quantitative measures are used exclusively in the assessment of effectiveness, implementation, and dissemination outcomes. In the aforementioned effectiveness trial of written resource navigation information plus patient navigation, Ell and colleagues (2009) assessed and compared treatment adherence rates between a group of low-income breast and gynecological cancer patients receiving the intervention and patients receiving enhanced usual care. Adherence to treatment—namely, external beam radiation or intravenous chemotherapy—was defined as completed as scheduled, completed but delayed because of missed treatment appointments, did not complete, or declined unless the interruption was physician prescribed or resulted from machine breakdown. In an RCT comparing an activating intervention, Brouwers and colleagues (Brouwers, De Bruijne, Terluin, Tiemens, & Verhaak, 2007) examined the cost-effectiveness of a structured treatment by social workers designed to reduce sick leave duration in patients due to emotional distress or minor mental disorders compared to usual general practitioner care. Outcomes included sick leave duration, clinical improvement over time, direct health care and intervention costs, indirect costs of production losses for paid labor, and difference in effects as measured by the mental and physical component scores of the Short Form-36 (a survey that measures functional health and well-being from the patient's perspective) and quality-adjusted life-years (QALYs) relative to direct and indirect costs.

All effectiveness trials assess client/patient functional status using standardized measures of physical and mental health and health behavior. For instance, Ell and colleagues (2010) assessed the effectiveness of an evidence-based, socioculturally adapted, collaborative depression care intervention for treatment of depression and diabetes using such outcome measures as the Symptom Checklist Depression Scale (SCL-20) (Derogatis, Lipman, Rickels, Uhlenhuth, & Covi, 1974), the Patient Health Questionnaire-9 (PHQ-9) (Wittkampf, Naeije, Schene, Huyser, & Van Weert, 2007), and the Medical Outcomes Study Short-Form Health Survey (SF-12) (Ware, Kosinski, & Keller, 1996).

Outcome measures in dissemination studies include measures of adoption and functional status. In a randomized trial evaluating three technical assistance strategies for disseminating a social-cognitive HIV risk reduction intervention model, Kelly and colleagues (2000) asked directors of AIDS service organizations at baseline and 6- and 12-month follow-up (1) whether small-group programs of at least 4 hours in duration and including all the core elements of the intervention had been offered to men who have sex with men or women in the past 6 months; (2) if so, how many times the program was offered in the past 6 months; and (3) whether a program including all of these elements had been offered to members of any other client populations. Atkins and colleagues (2008) assessed the impact of information dissemination through a network of key opinion leaders on adoption of recommended practices for children with attention-deficit/hyperactivity disorder in high-poverty urban schools using a 3-point scale ranging from 0 (no use) to 3 (highly successful use).

Implementation studies have also relied on quantitative measures of different outcomes. In a randomized effectiveness trial, Glisson and colleagues (2010) used the Child Behavior Checklist (CBCL) (Achenbach, 1991) to measure the outcome of a two-level strategy (implementation of MST for mental health treatment of delinquent youth and the Availability, Responsiveness, Continuity (ARC) organizational intervention to address service barriers). Jonkman and colleagues (2008) used ratings of implementation milestones and benchmarks by local coordinators, intervention staff, and trainers to compare implementation of the Communities That Care prevention operating system in the United States and the Netherlands.

Participant functional status outcomes have also been used in implementation studies. For instance, in a design that incorporates both effectiveness and implementation outcomes, Hawkins and colleagues (Hawkins, Brown, Oesterle, Arthur, Abbott, & Catalano, 2008; Brown et al., 2009) examined the impact of the Communities That Care prevention system on average levels of targeted risk factors and initiation of delinquent behavior and substance abuse in a panel of students followed from grades five through seven in CTC communities and control communities. Measures of these three outcomes were obtained from the Youth Development Survey (Social Development Research Group, 2005), a self-administered paper and pencil questionnaire designed to be administered in a 50-minute classroom period (Hawkins, Brown et al., 2008).

Quantitative measures of fidelity were also used in several studies based on the National Implementing Evidence-Based Practice Project for people with serious mental illness (McHugo et al., 2007; Marty et al., 2008; Brunette et al., 2008; Woltmann et al., 2008). The assessment of fidelity involved 1-day site visits to participating practices for the purpose of gathering information from various sources to make 5-point ratings on the critical components of the practice. A rating of 5 indicated full adherence to the model, while 1 indicated no adherence. The average of the item ratings yielded a total fidelity score. In the Community Youth Development Study, Fagan and colleagues developed instruments to measure four primary dimensions of implementation fidelity of the Communities That Care prevention operating system: (1) adherence to the program components and content, (2) dosage (i.e., number, length, and frequency of sessions), (3) quality of delivery, and (4) participant responsiveness (Fagan, Hanson, Hawkins, & Arthur, 2008).

Process and context data. In contrast to the almost exclusive reliance upon quantitative measures in assessing effectiveness, implementation, and dissemination outcomes, qualitative measures have been widely used to assess process and context. In effectiveness trials, qualitative methods have been used to obtain perspectives of both clients and providers. For instance, Griswold and colleagues (2008) conducted semistructured interviews with patients participating in a randomized trial of an intervention using care managers to understand patients' experiences with health care after a psychiatric crisis. Killaspy and colleagues (2009) conducted semistructured interviews with care coordinators to explore differences in approach to two types of community mental health treatment and to understand why clients exposed to assertive community treatment (ACT) were more satisfied and better engaged with services. Mitton and colleagues assessed client satisfaction with a community-based alternative to incarceration for mentally ill offenders using open-ended questions from a survey instrument (Mitton, Simpson, Gardner, Barnes, & McDougall, 2007).

Qualitative data have been used in assessments of dissemination process. For instance, Amodeo and colleagues described their experience testing Organization Development (OD) methods of dissemination of evidence-based practices in addiction treatment settings using a qualitative case study approach (Amodeo, Ellis, & Samet, 2006).

Qualitative methods have also been used to identify barriers and facilitators to implementation of evidence-based practices. For instance, Manuel and colleagues conducted a process and outcome evaluation of Bringing Evidence for Social Work Training (BEST)—an evidence-based supportive strategy to prepare social workers to use evidence-based practices—using data collected from focus groups conducted prior to and following the evidence-based practice training (Manuel, Mullen, Fang, Bellamy, & Bledsoe, 2009). Marty and colleagues (2008) examined barriers and facilitators to developing, implementing, and using outcome monitoring systems as part of the implementation efforts of 49 sites participating in the National Evidence-Based Practice Implementation Project. Implementation data were collected by implementation monitors (IMs) during monthly site visits. These data included observation of training sessions, leadership meetings, team meetings, and informal conversations with staff, families, and consumers. Semistructured interviews were also conducted with the evidence-based practice program leader and consultant trainer at each site every 6 months. These data were also used to assess barriers in one state that sought to implement supported employment and integrated dual-diagnosis treatment (Rapp et al., 2009). Another study used these data to explore the perceived effect of implementation on staff turnover (Woltmann et al., 2008).

Data Analyses

Quantitative Techniques. Assessment of outcomes in translational studies usually involve techniques ranging from descriptive and univariate techniques to those that require more complex modeling such as hierarchical linear modeling (HLM) (Raudenbush & Bryk, 2002), mixed-effects regression modeling (Hedeker & Gibbons, 2006), multilevel structural modeling (McArdle & Hamagami, 1996), or growth curve modeling (GCM) (Rogosa, Brandt, & Zimowski, 1982). Although randomization is conducted to eliminate the influence of confounders on outcomes by theoretically distributing both known and unknown variables equally among study groups, translational studies usually examine baseline demographics and clinical characteristics of study participants by independent t-test and analysis of variance for continuous variables and chi-square test for categorical variables to ensure that randomization has succeeded. Variables that are skewed in their distribution are either transformed before comparisons by intervention or examined using nonparametric statistics. When covariates differentiate treatment groups, it is necessary to include them in multivariate analyses to remove effects of confounding. It is also statistically useful to include covariates that explain outcome variance and do not differentiate between groups, because such variables increase statistical power.

To evaluate the effectiveness of an intervention or implementation strategy, logistic models are usually employed when evaluating categorical outcomes and repeated-measures analysis of variance or covariance, and general linear mixed effects models are used when evaluating continuous outcomes. Both models are adjusted for relevant demographic characteristics and baseline measures. For instance, Ell and colleagues (2010) used logistic regression models to compare the odds of achieving clinically meaningful improvement (greater than 50% decrease in depressive symptoms), remission of depressive symptoms, or persistent major depression between enhanced usual care and a socioculturally adapted collaborative depression care intervention at 6-, 12-, and 18-month follow-up. In the longitudinal cohort design of the Communities That Care project where the repeatedly measured outcomes are nested within students who, in turn, are nested within communities, with communities being nested within matched pairs of communities, Brown and colleagues relied on the general linear mixed model (McCulloch & Searle, 2001; Raudenbush & Bryk, 2002) for Gaussian distributed outcomes and the generalized linear mixed model (Liang & Zeger, 1986; Breslow & Clayton, 1993) with logit link transformation for Bernoulli distributed outcomes.

Survival analytical techniques, such as Cox regression modeling, may be used when attempting to evaluate the time it takes to achieve a specific outcome, such as the rate of adoption or dissemination of an evidence-based practice. Such techniques are especially useful when the amount of time that comparison groups have been under study varies and the primary outcome is right censored. By modeling how the hazard rate depends on intervention status and on other covariates, investigators can formally test for the intervention impact in a longitudinal design.

Missing Data. Common problems of experimental designs are missing data and loss to follow-up. For a variety of reasons, participants may be unwilling or unable to continue participation; even when subjects are willing and able, circumstances may preclude an investigator from monitoring outcomes over time. To address this problem, several strategies are used. Randomized trials usually adopt an intent-to-treat (ITT) analysis approach to evaluate intervention effects. The ITT approach to RCTs analyzes data on the basis of treatment assignment, not treatment receipt. Alternative approaches make comparisons according to the treatment received at the end of the trial (as-treated analysis) or only using subjects who did not deviate from the assigned treatment (adherers-only analysis). Using a sensitivity analysis on data for a hypothetical trial, Wright and Sim (2003) compared these different analytical approaches in the context of two common protocol deviations: loss to follow-up and switching across treatments. Their analysis showed that biased estimates of effect may occur when deviation is nonrandom, when a large percentage of participants switch treatments or are not subject to follow-up, and when the method of estimating missing values accounts inadequately for the process causing loss to follow-up. In general, ITT analysis attenuates between-group effects. The authors recommended use of sensitivity analyses on data and compare the characteristics of participants who do and do not deviate from the trial protocol. They conclude that the ITT approach is not a remedy for unsound design and that imputation of missing values is not a substitute for complete, good-quality data.

Another strategy for addressing loss to follow-up and missing data is to compare baseline characteristics of subjects available for analysis at each data point with those who are missing, to evaluate sampling biases. Analyses of trajectories of change observed in data collected at baseline and at the first follow-up data point may also provide information on the consequences of dropout on interpretation of outcomes. In addition, effects of dropout at any follow-up point may be clarified by comparing those included in the analyses and those missing at the next data point. If dropout (and early replacement of cases) occurs differentially or is deemed to be a possible source of bias in the analysis, additional analyses like propensity score stratification (Rosenbaum & Rubin, 1984) that specifically address sampling bias may be used.

Comparative Effectiveness Research. There have been increasing calls by the National Institutes of Health (NIH) and other funding and policymaking institutions for the examination of the comparative effectiveness of an evidence-based practice relative to usual care or another evidence-based practice (Federal Coordinating Council for Comparative Effectiveness Research, 2009; Social Work Policy Institute, 2010). Comparative effectiveness research assesses the benefits of an evidence-based practice relative to the costs of its implementation. The existing "gold standard" for economic assessment of medical interventions is cost per QALY. QALYs are measures of life expectancy in which years of life are appraised by quality of life (QOL) weights between 0 and 1, in which 0 is equivalent to death and 1 is equivalent to perfect health.

One of the goals of comparative effectiveness research is not only to determine whether an intervention produces a benefit on average or in a narrowly defined population but also in different groups of patients, distinguished by such characteristics as age, gender, race, severity of illness, the presence of comorbidities, and the presence of specific genetic markers. Comparative effectiveness research can also determine when a less-costly therapy offers equivalent or better health outcomes than an alternative or can support economic evaluations that seek to determine whether a more-effective and more-expensive alternative is worth the extra cost. In cases where an intervention is beneficial but costly and a decision maker wishes to consider costs, it is possible to calculate the net benefits of an intervention using either cost-benefit analysis, which values health in dollar terms and subtracts off costs, or a newer framework called net health benefits, which value health benefits in QALYs and subtracts off QALYs that could have been produced at the same cost as the intervention if they were used for some other, cost-effective, use (Garber & Meltzer, 2009, p. 17).

Qualitative Techniques. Qualitative analyses of the process and context of research translation typically involve an editing approach to data analysis in which researchers identify units in the text, forming the basis of data-developed categories, which are then used to reorganize the text so that its meaning can be clearly seen (Crabtree & Miller, 1992). One of the most commonly used methods for analyzing qualitative data in translational research is the "grounded theory" approach developed by Glaser and Strauss (1967). Grounded theory is theory derived from data and then illustrated by characteristic examples of data. One approach to grounded theory–based analysis, used in several translational studies (Aarons & Palinkas, 2007; Palinkas & Aarons, 2009; Palinkas et al., 2008), is outlined by Willms and colleagues (1990). Known as "Coding Consensus, Co-occurrence, and Comparison," analysis of field notes or interview transcripts begins with a review by the researcher(s) to develop a broad understanding of content as it relates to the project's specific aims and to identify topics of discussion and observation. During this step, as well as during subsequent steps, the investigator prepares short descriptive statements, or "memos," to document initial impressions of topics and themes and their relationships and to define the boundaries of specific codes (i.e., the inclusion and exclusion criteria for assigning a specific code). The empirical material contained in the interviews is then coded by researchers to condense the data into analyzable units. Segments of text ranging from a phrase to several paragraphs are assigned codes based on a priori (i.e., from an interview guide) or emergent themes (also known as open coding; Strauss & Corbin, 1998). Following the open coding, codes are assigned to describe connections between categories and between categories and subcategories (also known as axial coding; Strauss & Corbin, 1998). Codes may also be assigned to material to reflect the social and demographic characteristics of study participants. The final list of codes or codebook consists of a list of themes, issues, accounts of behaviors, and opinions that relate to the process and context of evaluation, implementation, or dissemination of an evidence-based practice. Based on these codes, a computer program such as NVivo or ATLAS.ti is used to generate a series of categories arranged in a treelike structure connecting text segments grouped into separate categories of codes, or "nodes." These nodes and trees are used to further the process of axial or pattern coding to examine the association between different a priori and emergent categories. They are also used in selective coding of material to identify the existence of new, previously unrecognized categories. Finally, through the process of constantly comparing these categories with each other, the different categories are further condensed into broad themes.

Another commonly used approach to qualitative analyses of process and context of evidence-based practice translation is the deductive–inductive method described by Miles and Huberman (1994). This approach was used in several studies based on the National Evidence-Based Practices Project and involved five key elements: (1) coding of data based on an a priori list of codes or topics, (2) condensation of data into reports, (3) use of rating scales to assess the importance or relevance of the data to the process and context of implementation, (4) development of themes based on the ratings that are examined out of context, and (5) a review of the summaries and key narratives to "recontextualize" the data and develop a list of key influences of implementation (Marshall et al., 2008).

Case Study

A currently funded clinical trial designed to examine the effectiveness of an evidence-based practice for treatment of externalizing behaviors by public youth-serving systems in California affords a unique opportunity to understand both outcomes and process of strategies designed to facilitate the implementation of an evidence based practice. "Using Community Development Teams to Scale-Up MTFC in California" (R01-MH076158) is a National Institute of Mental Health–funded, $5.5 million grant to inform translation of scientific evidence into health practice with Dr. Patricia Chamberlain as principal investigator. The youth-centered evidence-based practice being implemented is Multidimensional Treatment Foster Care (MTFC) (Chamberlain, Leve, & DeGarmo, 2007), an evidence-based program for out-of-home youth aged 8 to 18 with emotional or behavioral problems. MTFC has been shown to reduce out-of-home placement in group and residential care, juvenile arrests, substance abuse, youth violence, and behavioral and emotional problems.

The implementation method being tested is the use of Community Development Teams (CDTs; Sosna & Marsenich, 2006). The CDT model was developed in 2001 by the California Institute of Mental Health to facilitate the implementation of evidence-based practices in California. The CDT operates through multicounty development team meetings that are augmented by county-individualized technical assistance. Key stakeholders in each county are drawn from multiple levels (i.e., consumers, system leaders, organizations/agencies, and practitioners) to participate in development team meetings that cover the following: (a) information about specific evidence-based practices and their fit with state and county needs and policies; (b) peer-to-peer exchanges identifying barriers, planning for implementation, and examining data for fidelity monitoring; and (c) support and feedback about progress and problems encountered throughout the adoption, implementation, fidelity monitoring, and sustainability process. The CDT meetings provide structured and informal interactions between and within counties to help find solutions to barriers, provide reinforcement/redirection of efforts, focus toward improvement in adherence, and resolve conflict, as needed.

The MTFC Implementation Study uses 40 California counties and 11 Ohio counties that have not already adopted MTFC. Using a cluster randomization design as described earlier, these states were matched to form four nearly equivalent groups: three in California and one in Ohio. Control sites obtain technical assistance for implementing MTFC from Treatment Foster Care Consultants, Inc. (TFCC) without the use of CDTs, referred to as the standard intervention (SI). The matched groups in California were also randomly assigned to three sequential cohorts in a wait-list design with staggered start-up timelines (at months 6, 18, or 30). Within each of the four cohorts, counties were randomly assigned to CDT or standard implementation conditions, thereby generating eight replicate groups of counties with four assigned to CDT. Random assignment to cohorts determined the timeline for their participation in the interventions. This wait-listed design allowed investigators to attend to training only one third of the counties at a time. Participating counties receive all of the consulting and technical assistance usually offered by TFCC to sites wishing to implement MTFC. Within the 51 counties are approximately 600 system leaders, agency directors, and practitioners; 400 foster parents; and 900 youth and their families.

Assessment of Outcomes

The primary aim of this project is to test whether CDT improves program adoption, implementation, and fidelity. Comparing CDT against SI, investigators are examining (a) the proportion of counties that adopt MTFC and the rate of adoption, (b) the stage of MTFC implementation that counties reach and their implementation rate, and (c) the fidelity of implementation, including model adherence and practitioner competence (Chamberlain et al., 2008). Also under investigation is whether fixed contextual factors (i.e., poverty, urban/rural setting, being a federal system of care county, consumer advocacy, history of collaboration) moderate this intervention effect. The primary outcome is the Stages of Implementation Checklist (SIC) (Chamberlain et al., 2008). Multiple indicators are used to measure both the progression through the stage and quality of participation of the individuals involved at each stage. Stages 1 to 3 track the site's decision to adopt or not adopt MTFC, feasibility, readiness, and adequacy of implementation planning. In stage 4, recruitment and training of the MTFC treatment staff (i.e., program supervisor, family therapist, individual therapist, foster parent trainer/recruiter, and behavioral skills trainer) and foster parents are measured. Stage 5 tracks the training and implementation of procedures to measure fidelity of MTFC use. Stage 6 tracks services and consultation with services, including dates of first placement, consult call, clinical meeting, and foster parent meeting. Stage 7 tracks ongoing services, consultation, and fidelity monitoring and how sites use that data to improve adherence. Stage 8 evaluates the site's competency in the domains required for certification as an independent MTFC program. During stages 1 through 3, the county mental health director is the respondent; during the remaining stages, the organization/agency director is the respondent.

Assessment of Process

In addition to assessing outcomes, the project is designed to examine the process of implementation and the influence of dynamic contextual factors on this process. The study examines the following dynamic factors hypothesized to mediate positive outcomes: organizational culture and climate (Glisson, 1992), system and practitioner attitudes toward evidence-based practices (Aarons, 2004), and adherence to competing treatment models or philosophies (Judge, Thoresen, Pucik, & Welbourne, 1999). These dynamic factors are expected to influence how well MTFC is accepted and integrated into implementing agencies (Chamberlain et al., 2008). The mediation hypothesis is that these dynamic factors will change with exposure to the CDT and that these changes will mediate the effects of the CDT on outcomes realized by the counties. However, it is also hypothesized that regardless of study condition (i.e., SI or CDT), counties with high scores on these dynamic factors (as measured by a set of standardized instruments) will proceed further and faster through the stages of implementation than will counties that have low scores (Chamberlain et al., 2008).

Embedded within this implementation trial was a mixed-methods study, funded by the William T. Grant Foundation, focused on the process and context of implementation of MTFC. Using a combination of qualitative and quantitative methods, this project had three specific aims: (1) to describe the structure and operation of influence networks of public youth–serving systems in 12 California counties comprising the first cohort of the MTFC Implementation Study; (2) to determine the influence of these networks on decisions related to study participation, and (3) to identify the personal and contextual factors that influenced the operation of these networks within the context of the MTFC Implementation Study. Semistructured interviews were conducted, either in person or via telephone, with the directors and senior administrators of child welfare, mental health, and probation departments in 12 of the 13 counties that were recruited to participate in the first cohort of the MTFC Implementation Study (N = 38). The semistructured interview centered on knowledge and implementation of MTFC and other evidence-based practices at the county level. Interviewees were asked if they had ever heard of the MTFC Implementation Study or MTFC and what their motivations were to participate or not participate in the program. Participants were then asked who they had talked to about participation in MTFC or other evidence-based practices; prompts were given to participants as necessary to identify whom they talked to, their relationship to that person, their reasons for talking to that person, and the amount of influence that person had on their decision to participate in MTFC or a similar evidence-based practice. Then participants were asked about collaborations both within and between county agencies (child welfare, mental health, probation) and the nature of these collaborations. Specifically, participants were asked to identify what made for a successful versus an unsuccessful collaboration. Finally, participants were asked about who usually suggested that their agency take on new programs or initiatives. Probes for influence network actors included agency staff, other agencies, community-based organizations, other county officials, etc.

A web-based survey was also sent to each of the agency directors and the program managers/clinicians. The survey asked participants to provide general demographic information (i.e., gender, age, number of years in occupation, current position, and time with agency). Per criteria established by Valente (1995), each study participant was asked to identify up to 10 individuals on whom they relied on for advice about whether and how to use evidence-based practices to meet the mental health needs of youth served by their agency. The matrix of ties used to analyze advice networks was constructed from data collected from the web-based survey, supplemented by data collected during the qualitative interviews. The social network analysis proceeded in three stages: network visualization, structural analysis, and statistical analysis of outcomes. The network visualization was accomplished using NetDraw 2.090. Structural analyses were then conducted on these network data using Ucinet for Windows, Version 6 (Borgatti, Everett, & Freeman, 2002). Several network-level measures of structure were assessed, including total number of ties, network size, density (the number of reported links divided by the maximum number of possible links), average distance between nodes, and the number of components (i.e., unique subnetworks). To assess status in the network, researchers calculated degree centrality for both incoming ties (being nominated by alters) and outgoing ties (nominating alters). In-degree and out-degree centrality scores assess the relative status of a given node.

Systems leaders develop and maintain networks of information and advice-based on roles, responsibility, geography, and friendship ties (Palinkas, Fuentes, Holloway, Wu, & Chamberlain, 2010). Networks expose leaders to information about and opportunities to adopt evidence-based practices or interventions ; they also influence decisions to adopt these practices. Individuals in counties at the same stage of implementation accounted for 83% of all network ties. Networks in counties that decided not to implement a specific evidence-based practice had no extra-county ties. Implementation of evidence-based practices was associated with the size of county, urban versus rural counties, and in-degree centrality. Collaboration is viewed as critical to implementing evidence-based practices, especially in small, rural counties where agencies have limited resources on their own.

One of the conclusions to be drawn from this research is that implementation studies should consider the existence of naturally occurring networks of participants when designing RCTs. Small counties implement evidence-based practices based on the economies of scale. They are more willing to engage in clinical trials and/or implement new programs if they can partner with neighboring counties, usually because they lack the demand for such programs (too few clients) or the ability to meet that demand (i.e., staff and infrastructure to support the evidence-based practice).

Challenges in Conducting Research

There exist several challenges in conducting translational research on process and outcomes of evidence-based practice effectiveness, dissemination, and implementation. First, key processes involved in the translation of evidence-based practices must be modeled and measured. However, as Proctor and colleagues (2009) note, each form of translation may require specific constructs and procedures for the measurement of those concepts. For instance, "implementation research requires outcomes that are conceptually and empirically distinct from those of service and treatment effectiveness. These include the intervention's penetration within a target organization, its acceptability to and adoption by multiple stakeholders, the feasibility of its use, and its sustainability over time with the service system setting" (p. 30).

Second, because translation is a process, measurement of translation components must take into consideration the dynamic nature of this process. Service systems are not static entities; they undergo changes due to turnover in staff and leadership, policy initiatives, funding opportunities or budget constraints, and consumer demand for services. Similarly, evidence-based practices themselves experience change to accommodate the operational constraints of organizations, preferences of providers, or the specific sociocultural or clinical characteristics of consumers. Under these circumstances, what is being assessed may change from one study to the next, from one organization to the next, and perhaps even from one consumer or client to the next.

Third, because translation typically occurs in complex systems of service delivery where the unit of translation is not a single consumer or even a single provider but an organization or group of organizations, assessment of translation processes often possess limited statistical power due to the small sample size. Even if funds are available to increase the number of units engaged in the effectiveness, dissemination, or implementation of an evidence-based practice, there may simply be too few organizations available to include in a research project. As Proctor and colleagues (2009, p. 29) note, "systematic studies of implementation require creative multi-level designs to address the challenges of sample size estimation; by definition, larger system levels carry sample sizes with lower potential power estimates than do individual level analyses." Mixed-effects quantitative models are limited in addressing small samples, requiring use of mixed-methods designs as will be discussed in Chapter 6.

The fourth challenge is one of engagement of all relevant stakeholders in the translational research enterprise. Social service agencies and providers may be unwilling to participate in translational research of an evidence-based practice for several reasons, including an unwillingness to learn new practices, especially those that may be inconsistent with the agency or practitioner treatment philosophy, an unwillingness to abandon old patterns of care, and a lack of leader support for the practice. Researchers may be similarly unwilling to compromise on agency or provider suggestions for evidence-based practice adaptation in the belief that it will both weaken the effectiveness of the evidence-based practice and weaken external validity of what is actually being measured. Consumers may be reluctant to adhere to new practices that are inconsistent with their own understanding of appropriate and desired forms of service delivery. Minorities, in particular, may be reluctant to engage in any research activity for fear of exploitation and discrimination.

Related to the challenge of engagement, a fifth challenge to conducting translational research is associated with the use of the

RCT design. Circumstances may preclude the use of the RCT design, including the ethics of providing service to one group and denying the same service to another group of clients, the expense and logistics involved in conducting such research, and the unwillingness of participants or organizations to accept randomization. According to Glasgow and colleagues, nonrandomized designs may be desired when external validity is very important and the intervention takes many forms and levels of quality, the diversity of the population requires multiple adaptations, or the intervention is part of a complex, multilevel approach requiring adaptations (Glasgow, Magid, Beck, Ritzwoller, & Estabrooks, 2005). "In many clinical and community settings, and especially in studies with underserved populations and low resource settings, randomization may not be feasible or acceptable" (p. 554). For instance, in the case study discussed earlier in this chapter, Palinkas (2009) found that randomization of counties into cohorts failed to take into consideration the existence of natural networks of advice and support. Such networks could either maximize the effect on an implementation intervention designed to develop such support networks or it might attenuate the effects by working with non–naturally occurring networks. In such circumstances, alternatives to the randomized design such as "interrupted time series," "multiple baselines across settings," or "regression-discontinuity" designs may be advisable.

Landsverk and colleagues recommended the use of designs that "mimic the element of choice by consumers and providers in community service settings targeted for implementation of evidence-based practices" (Landsverk, Brown, Reutz, Palinkas, & Horwitz, 2011). They cite as examples a set of randomized designs that are considerably more complex than traditional RCTs but also more sensitive to issues of external validity. These include a randomized encouragement trial (RET) that randomizes consumers to encouragement strategies for the targeted treatment and facilitates their preferences and choices under naturalistic clinical practice settings (West et al., 2008); the Sequential Multiple Assignment Randomized Trial (SMART), a clinical trial design that experimentally examines strategy choices, accommodates patient and provider preferences for treatment while using adaptive randomization strategies, and allows multiple comparison options (Murphy, Lynch, Oslin, McKay, & Ten Have, 2007; Ten Have, Coyne, Salzer, & Katz, 2003; Ten Have, Joffe, & Cary, 2003); and the randomized fractional factorial design, which screens more efficiently and tests multiple treatment components with less cost (Collins, Murphy, Nair, & Strecher, 2005).

Finally, the availability of sustained support represents a significant challenge for translational research. Effectiveness, dissemination, and implementation trials are constantly faced with the prospect that the evidence-based practices that are the focus of such research may not be sustainable once the research project has been completed. Although such trials generally are required to provide some indication of likely sustainability, the availability of non–research-related funding to support evidence-based practices is generally beyond the control of researchers and dependent upon broader political and economic forces that govern service delivery. Shifts in public priorities may result in the elimination of funding and the disappearance of tested programs regardless of the evidence supporting their effectiveness. Translational research must be conducted with this prospect in mind.

Infrastructure Requirements

Engaging in translational research requires attention to staffing, research–community relationships, and participant compensation.

Staffing

The staffing of translational research projects should be multidisciplinary, multimethod and multilevel in nature. Such projects require both clinical and theoretical expertise, the latter often represented by individuals with training in different disciplines and theoretical traditions. Among the disciplines represented in implementation studies, for instance, are social workers, clinical and organizational psychologists, sociologists and anthropologists, economists and political scientists, and experts in business and management. Multimethod expertise is also essential to the conduct of translational research. As noted earlier, assessment of outcomes requires expertise in quantitative methods while assessment of process usually requires expertise in qualitative methods. Within each methodological tradition, specific skill sets may be required, such as an understanding of the principles and application of mixed-effects models to evaluate outcomes or grounded theory to evaluate process. Finally, staffing should be multilevel with expertise to manage and supervise projects and expertise to provide specific tasks such as data collection, management, and analysis, as well as logistical support.

Researcher–Community Relationships

Because research translation is inherently based in the community, the infrastructure to support the development and maintenance of research–community partnerships to engage in translational research is also critical. This infrastructure is guided by the principles and practice of community-based participatory research, as will be examined in Chapter 7. It also requires resources to sustain such partnerships, including technology to facilitate communication and engagement among research partners; identification and training of personnel to facilitate such communication; training of community partners in research methods and research partners in community practices; and means of disseminating research findings.

Participant Compensation

Finally, translational research requires resources to compensate research subjects. Services research projects generally take into consideration the compensation of individual participants for participating in a survey or undergoing a clinical procedure through cash payments, vouchers, or prize lotteries. However, compensation to organizations and their staff is equally important to facilitate continued engagement and investment in the project. Such compensation serves as a form of acknowledgment of the importance of the organization to the project and allows staff the opportunity to devote time and energy to the research without incurring personal expense or expense to their employer.

Additional Resources

For additional information on the design and execution of RCTs of behavioral interventions:

Brown, C. H., Wang, W., Kellam, S. G., Muthén, B. O., Petras, H., Toyinbo, P., . . . the Prevention Science and Methodology Group. (2008). Methods for testing theory and evaluating impact in randomized field trials: Intent-to-treat analyses for integrating the perspectives of person, place, and time. *Drug and Alcohol Dependence, 95*(Suppl. 1)**,** S74–S104. doi: 10.1016/j.drugalcdep.2007.11.013

Poduska, J., Kellam, S., Brown, C. H., Ford, C., Windham, A., Keegan, N., & Wang, W. (2009). Study protocol for a group randomized controlled trial of a classroom-based intervention aimed at preventing early risk factors for drug abuse: Integrating effectiveness and implementation research. *Implementation Science,* 4(56). doi:10.1186/17485908456

For additional information on alternatives to randomized controlled trial designs:

Brown, C. H., Ten Have, T. R., Jo, B., Dagne, G., Wyman, P. A., Muthén, B., & Gibbons R. D. (2009). Adaptive designs for randomized trials in public health. *Annual Review of Public Health, 30*, 1–25.

For additional information on comparative effectiveness research:

Social Work Policy Institute. (2010). *Comparative effectiveness research and social work: Strengthening the connection.* Retrieved from http://www.socialworkpolicy.org/wp-content/uploads/2010/03/SWPI-CER-Full-RPT-FINAL.pdf

5

Research on Organizational Context

This chapter considers the methodological challenges and strategies at one specific level of the translation process: the organizational level. Organizational factors include organizational structure, culture and climate, work attitudes, leadership, social influences, and readiness or support for innovation. Such factors can increase or decrease the likelihood that new evidence-based practices or interventions will be disseminated and implemented as intended (Frambach & Schillewaert, 2002; Klein & Sorra, 1996). The organizational level also provides an ideal focus for examining the context of research translation in two respects. First, it serves as the context in which individual providers and practitioners deliver evidence-based practices. Second, service organizations themselves reside within a broader context of external influences on practice, including policies and mandates, government funding, and client demand.

Principles and Practice of Research

Conceptual Frameworks

Research on the translation and implementation of evidence-based practices has focused on four distinct levels of services delivery (Ferlie & Shortell, 2001; Grol & Grimshaw, 1999; Schoenwald, 2009): (1) the larger service system or environment, (2) the implementing organization; (3) groups or teams of individuals delivering the practice (practitioners); and (4) the individual providers and consumers of the service. The first level has been referred to by Greenhalgh and colleagues (2004) and others (c.f., Horwitz, Chamberlain, Landsverk, & Mullican, 2010) as the "outer context" of research translation, while the remaining three levels have been referred to as the "inner context." According to Schoenwald (2009, p. 236),

> Interventions designed to effect change at any one level are likely to be multifaceted, and may differ from those capable of effecting change at another level (Grol & Grimshaw, 1999; Schoenwald & Henggeler, 2004). At the service system level, for example, coercive strategies such as regulations, legal mandates, and budget manipulation can be effective in establishing a "floor" or "ceiling" for local variations in practice (Ferlie & Shortell, 2001). At the practitioner level, however, a combination of educational, behavioral, and social influence strategies might be needed to facilitate learning and application of a new treatment model. At the organizational level, strategies used to develop effective "implementation policies" (Klein & Knight, 2005) might be needed to "restructure care processes" to build a specific innovation into routines (Grol & Grimshaw, 1999). A different set of strategies might be needed to cultivate support for innovation in the organization more generally (Glisson & Schoenwald, 2005; Lehman, Greener, & Simpson, 2002).

The set of strategies appropriate to each level, in turn, may call for a different set of methods for their design and evaluation. Real and Poole (2005), for instance, note that there are limitations to drawing conclusions about one level with data gathered at another level.

While any or all of the four levels would provide some understanding of the process and outcomes of research translation, the argument for focusing on the organizational level is best articulated by Glisson and colleagues as follows:

> One reason that organizations are believed to play a central role in service effectiveness in a variety of human service arenas is that they establish a social context of shared service provider expectations, perceptions and attitudes that affect

the adoption and implementation of evidence-based practices, the nature of the relationships that develop between service provider and consumers, and the overall availability, responsiveness, and continuity of the services (Aarons and Palinkas, 2007; Grol & Grimshaw, 2003; Nelson & Steele, 2007; Nelson et al., 2006). Therefore, variations in organization-based social contexts may explain in part the gap between what we know about treatment efficacy and about how to best deliver effective treatments in the community. For this reason, a well developed science of implementation effectiveness requires a better understanding of organizational social context and of methods for measuring and incorporating organizational social context into community-based effectiveness studies. Theory and research in several fields suggest the social context of a mental health service organization plays an important role in creating and sustaining the shared expectations, perceptions and attitudes of the clinicians who provide mental health services (Aarons & Palinkas, 2007; Glisson, 2002; Nelson & Steele, 2007; Nelson et al., 2006). The expectations (e.g., the extent to which clinicians are expected to be proficient in their work), perceptions (e.g., whether clinicians perceive a high level of personal engagement in their work with clients), and attitudes (e.g., clinicians commitment to the organization in which they work) are believed to either encourage or inhibit the adoption of best practices, strengthen or weaken fidelity to established protocols, support or attenuate positive relationships between service providers and consumers, and increase or decrease the availability, responsiveness and continuity of services provided by the organization (Glisson, Landsverk et al., 2008, pp. 98–99).

Organizational Influences on Evidence-Based Practice Implementation

In social work, there have been three lines of research examining the relationships between characteristics of organizations and the translation of research into practice. The first line of research has focused on the influence of organizational characteristics on the implementation of evidence-based practicess. Most of this research has centered on the culture and climate of organizations. *Organizational culture* can be defined as the implicit norms, values, shared behavioral expectations, and assumptions of a work unit that guide behaviors (Cooke & Rousseau, 1988). This culture "emerges from that which is shared between colleagues in an organization, including shared beliefs, attitudes, values, and norms of behavior. This organizational culture is reflected by a common way of making sense of the organization that allows people to see situations and events in similar and distinctive ways. It is 'the way things are done around here,' as well as the way things are understood, judged, and valued" (Davies, Nutley, & Mannion, 2000, p. 112). As with cultural systems in general, organizational cultures are comprised of sets of shared understandings arranged in hierarchical order.

At the most basic level are the underlying assumptions that represent the unconscious and "taken for granted" beliefs that structure the thinking and behavior of an individual. These assumptions give rise to organizational values that operate at a more conscious level and represent the standards and goals to which individuals attribute intrinsic worth. Then, more visible still are the artifacts that represent the concrete manifestations of culture. These might include, for example, the ceremonies, traditions, and incentive structures peculiar to an organization (Davies et al., 2000, p. 112).

Organizational culture can affect how readily new practices will be considered and adopted in practice (Hemmelgarn, Glisson, & Dukes, 2001; Simpson, 2002). In human services, organizational culture influences case manager attitudes, perceptions, and behaviors (Glisson & James, 2002). Aarons and Sawitzky (2006) found that a constructive organizational culture of programs providing mental health services for youth and families was associated with positive attitudes of providers toward adoption of EBP. Manuel and colleagues (2009) found a lack of agency culture encouraging and supporting EBP implementation to be a significant barrier to implementing the Bringing Evidence to Social Work Training (BEST) intervention. Glisson and colleagues (2008) found organizational culture to be a significant independent predictor of new program sustainability.

Using data collected from a nationwide survey of 200 community mental health center directors, Schoenwald and colleagues (2008) examined the association between factors important to the implementation of new treatments and governance structures, financing structures and reimbursement, and provider organizations. Results of random-effects regression models (RRMs) evaluating associations between governance, financing, and organizational characteristics and the use of new treatments and services showed for-profit organizations were more likely to implement such treatments, and organizations with more licensed clinical staff and weekly clinical supervision in place less likely to do so. This study also found three factors of greater importance to public organizations than private organizations—fit with existing implementation practices, infrastructure support, and organizational mission and support.

Likewise, the attitudes and leadership styles of agency directors may influence the process of research translation. Aarons (2006) found both transformational (charismatic or visionary) and transactional (based on exchanges between leader and follower) leadership to be positively associated with a more positive attitude toward adoption of EBP, and transformational leadership was negatively associated with the perception of a difference between current practice and EBP. Brunette and colleagues (2008) found administrative leadership to be significantly associated with implementation of integrated dual disorders treatment in community mental health settings. Along with partnerships with universities, Proctor and colleagues (2007) found director leadership and support for providers to be important leverage points to implement evidence-based treatments in such settings.

Organizational climate refers to employee perceptions and affective responses to the work environment (Joyce & Slocom, 1984; Sells & James, 1988). Climate includes characteristics of the job (e.g., autonomy, variety, feedback, role clarity) and the work group (e.g., cooperation, warmth/intimacy) (Glisson, 1989).

> Climate can be defined at two levels. At the individual level, *psychological* climate is the individual's perception of the psychological impact of the work environment on his or her own well-being (James & James, 1989). If employees in the same work unit share the same perceptions, their perceptions can be aggregated to describe the organizational climate of that unit (Jones & James, 1979; Joyce & Slocum, 1984). However, organizational climate remains a property of the individuals because it represents the individuals' shared perceptions of how their work environment impacts them as individuals (James, 1982) (Glisson et al., 2006, p. 858).

Glisson and Hemmelgarn (1998) and Schoenwald and colleagues (Schoenwald, Sheidow, Letourneau, & Liao, 2003) demonstrated that organizational climate significantly affected clinical outcomes for youth in publicly funded human services. Staff turnover, a consequence of poor organizational climate, was identified by Brunette and colleagues (2008) as a barrier to the implementation of integrated dual-disorders treatment in community mental health settings. Climate for innovation is also important in understanding openness to change among human service organizations (Anderson & West, 1998; Klein & Sorra, 1996) and is associated with provider attitudes toward adopting evidence-based practices (Aarons & Sawitzky, 2006).

Attitudes toward organizational change, determined in part by the culture and climate of the organization, have been found to be important in the dynamics of innovation. Combined with the social and demographic characteristics of the organization's staff and leadership (e.g., age, gender, education, professional status), organizational culture and climate influence the process of research translation by influencing attitudes toward EBP (Aarons, 2004). Other organizational characteristics that promote the implementation of evidence-based practices include an organization's absorptive capacity, readiness for change, and receptive context (Horwitz et al., 2010). According to Horwitz and colleagues (2010, p. 34), "organizations that start with good knowledge/skills, can incorporate new knowledge, are highly specialized and have mechanisms in place to spread knowledge throughout the organization, are much more likely to explore evidence-based practices and eventually initiate them (Ferlie & Shortell, 2001; Grol et al., 2007; Damanpour, 1991; Greenhalgh et al., 2004)."

Another characteristic of organizations is *work attitudes*, a characteristic of individual members of an organization that includes job satisfaction and organizational commitment (Glisson & Durick, 1988). Whereas job satisfaction is a positive appraisal of one's own job or job experiences, organizational commitment as a willingness to exert considerable personal effort on behalf of one's organization and a strong desire to remain a member of the organization (Mowday, Porter, & Steers, 1982). High employee morale is a function of both satisfaction and commitment (Glisson, Landsverk et al., 2008).

Finally, although many factors influence the diffusion of evidence-based practices, researchers have consistently found that *interpersonal contacts* within and between organizations and communities are important influences on the adoption of new behaviors (Brekke et al., 2007; Palinkas, Allred, & Landsverk, 2005; Rogers, 2003). Based on Diffusion of Innovations Theory (Rogers, 2003) and Social Learning Theory (Bandura, 1986), Valente's (1995) social network thresholds model calls for identification and matching of champions within peer networks that manage organizational agenda setting, change, and evaluation of change (e.g., data collection, evaluation, and feedback) and use information technology processes consistent with continuous quality improvement strategies. Studies and meta-analyses have shown that both the influence of trusted others in one's personal network and having access and exposure to external information are important influences on rates of adoption of innovative practices (Valente, 2010).

Impact of Research Translation on Organizations

The second line of research examining the association between characteristics of social work organizations and research translation has focused on the impacts of translation on the organization. Several studies have focused on how the implementation of evidence-based practices might adversely affect organizations by adding to the workload of an already overworked labor force or by leading to increased employee turnover as social workers long used to providing services in a particular way are called upon to change their practices and adopt new ones that might restrict their sense of control over the therapeutic process (Glisson, Schoenwald et al., 2008; Sheidow, Schoenwald, Wagner, Allred, & Burns, 2007; Woltmann et al., 2008). Other studies have focused on the benefits to organizations that have occurred with evidence-based practice implementation; these include an enhanced professional identity, improved client outcomes, and gratification of contributing to a process of knowledge generation (Aarons & Palinkas, 2007; Palinkas & Aarons, 2009). Evidence-based practice implementation has also resulted in improved organizational performance; however, these improvements are dependent upon certain organizational factors such as preimplementation inertia and efficiency (Hovmand & Gillespie, 2008).

Organization-Level Implementation Strategies

The third line of research examining the association between characteristics or organizations and evidence-based practice implementation has been the use of organizational interventions to facilitate the adoption and routine use of such practices. Several strategies currently being examined are designed to facilitate the implementation of evidence-based practices in social work settings. These include the ARC model described in Chapter 3, the use of Community Development Teams to implement Multidimensional Treatment Foster Care described in the case study in Chapter 4, and the Communities That Care prevention implementation model developed by Hawley and colleagues that will be introduced in Chapter 7.

In each of these instances, the strategies target specific organizational factors, including attitudes toward evidence-based practices and readiness to innovate (the ARC model), community-based administration and leadership (the CTC model), and social relations and interactions (the CDT model). Other organization-level strategies have been used to implement evidence-based practices. Barwick and colleagues (Barwick, Peters, & Boydell, 2009), for instance, evaluated the benefits of a community of practice (CoP) model (Lave & Wenger, 1991) in implementing a standardized outcome measure to monitor client response to treatment in the context of Ontario's child mental health sector. A CoP is a group of people who share knowledge, learn together, and create common practices. In this study, readiness for change, practice change, content knowledge, and satisfaction with and use of implementation supports were examined among practitioners newly trained on the measure and who were randomly assigned to a CoP or practice-as-usual group. Results revealed no difference between groups in readiness for change or reported practice change but did show a greater use of the tool in practice, better content knowledge, and more satisfaction with implementation supports among the CoP group.

Organization-level interventions have also been applied to facilitate evidence-based practice dissemination. Amodeo and colleagues (2006) tested Organizational Development (OD) methods (French & Bell, 1998) for dissemination of evidence-based practices in two addiction treatment programs, developing organization-specific treatment plans using employee work teams with a goal of changing organizational policies and procedures and improving practitioner skills. Although OD was considered to be effectively applied, the practices were considered to be premature for these programs because more fundamental aspects of client–clinician interaction and agency treatment philosophy needed to be addressed before implementation. Atkins and colleagues (2008) evaluated the effectiveness of key opinion leaders (KOLs) in disseminating recommended practices for children with attention-deficit/hyperactivity disorder (ADHD) in high-poverty urban schools. Schools were selected from a pool of 64 high-poverty Chicago public schools and randomly assigned to the KOL (n = 6) or comparison (n = 4) condition. Mixed-effects regression models showed that KOLs in collaboration with mental health providers promoted higher rates of teachers' self-reported use of recommended strategies than mental health providers alone and that these effects were mediated by KOL support but not by mental health provider support.

Methods for Conducting Organization-Level Translational Research

Research Designs

Consistent with translational research in general, research at the organization level involves observational, quasi-experimental, and experimental designs and the use of quantitative, qualitative, and mixed methods. Observational designs have been used to assess characteristics of organizations that facilitate or inhibit evidence-based practice implementation (e.g., Glisson, Schoenwald et al., 2008; Manuel et al., 2009; Marty et al., 2008; Proctor et al., 2007). Quasi-experimental (Amodeo et al., 2006) and experimental (Atkins et al., 2008; Barwick et al., 2009; Brown et al., 2009; Chamberlain et al., 2008; Wells et al., 2000) designs have been used to assess the effectiveness of strategies designed to facilitate implementation by using or modifying characteristics of organizations. Observational studies have used both cross-sectional and longitudinal designs, while experimental designs of organizational change are inherently longitudinal.

Quantitative Methods

The organization-level studies described in this chapter and throughout this book relied on quantitative or qualitative methods or both. Quantitative studies have focused on the application of instruments for measuring specific organizational factors, including culture and climate, workplace attitudes, and social relations. One of the most commonly used measures of organizational culture and climate in social services organizations is the Children's Services Survey (Glisson, 2002). The organizational culture scales in this instrument were derived from the Organizational Culture Inventory (Cooke & Rousseau, 1988) and adapted for use in mental health services (Glisson & James, 2002). Reliabilities range from 0.86 to 0.89 for constructive culture subscales and from 0.75 to 0.86 for defensive culture subscales (Glisson & James, 2002). The organizational climate scales are based on organizational studies in diverse workplace settings (Mowday et al., 1982) and assess dimensions such as depersonalization, emotional exhaustion, and role conflict with reliabilities ranging from 0.69 to 0.92 (Glisson & James, 2002). Lower scores on these scales indicate more positive climate and higher scores indicate a more negative organizational climate.

A relatively new measure of organizations is the Organizational Social Context scale (OSC) (Glisson, Landsverk et al., 2008), which examines the rigidity, proficiency, and resistance in organizational cultures and engagement, functionality, and stress of organizational climates. Glisson and colleagues assessed the psychometric properties of the OSC measure in a nationwide study of 1,154 clinicians in 100 mental health clinics with a second-order confirmatory factor analysis of clinician responses, estimates of scale reliabilities, and indices of within-clinic agreement and between-clinic differences among clinicians (Glisson, Landsverk et al., 2008).

Another widely used measure is the Evidence-Based Practice Attitudes Scale (EBPAS) (Aarons, 2004). The EBPAS is a brief (15-item) measure that assesses individual provider attitudes toward adoption of innovation in mental health services. The EBPAS assesses four dimensions of attitudes toward adoption of EBP: (1) intuitive *appeal* of EBP, (2) likelihood of adopting EBP given *requirements* to do so, (3) *openness* to new practices, and (4) perceived *divergence* between research-based/academically developed interventions and current practice. The EBPAS has established reliability and validity with an overall Cronbach's alpha of .77. Aarons and colleagues recently expanded the EBPAS to create a new 50-item version (EBPAS-50) by combining the original 15 items with 35 new items identified from a mixed-methods analysis that identified eight new factors with moderate-to-large factor loadings and fair-to-excellent internal consistency reliabilities (Aarons, Cafri, Lugo, & Sawitzky, 2010).

Qualitative Methods

Qualitative methods have also been used primarily to examine organization-level barriers and facilitators to research translation. For instance, Proctor and colleagues (2007) conducted semistructured interviews with seven community mental health clinic directors to identify barriers and facilitators to implementing evidence-based practices in such settings. Directors identified limited access to research, provider resistance, and training costs as barriers to implementation, while director leadership, support to providers, and partnerships with universities were identified as facilitators. Manuel and colleagues (2009) conducted focus groups to evaluate the process and outcomes of implementing the BEST intervention.

Still other studies have relied on a combination of qualitative and quantitative methods. For instance, a study by Gioia and Dziadosz (2008) used the EBPAS to assess changes in attitudes toward evidence-based practices associated with the adoption of five different evidence-based practices in a single large mental health agency. Semistructured interviews were conducted to obtain firsthand accounts of practitioners' experience with training within the agency. The two sets of data were used to examine the process of implementation and to identify barriers and facilitators in this process.

Case Study

Oklahoma Children's Services (OCS) is a community-based home-visiting family preservation and reunification service system for child welfare cases that operates on a regionalized, contracted basis. It serves approximately 1,500 new child welfare–referred families annually. In collaboration with investigators at the University of Oklahoma Health Sciences Center (Mark Chaffin, principal investigator), OCS implemented an evidence-based protocol, the SafeCare

(SC) model (also known in Oklahoma as the ecobehavioral [EB] model), with ongoing technical assistance and training support provided by the CDC Division of Violence Prevention. Originally known as Project 12-Ways (Lutzker & Bigelow, 2002; Lutzker & Rice, 1984), this model was designed primarily for families involved in the child welfare system due to neglect, physical abuse, or both, although most intervention components are focused on child neglect. It is geared toward families with preschool or school-age children. The model is manualized and structured and uses classic behavioral intervention techniques (e.g., ongoing measurement of observable behaviors, skill modeling, direct skill practice with feedback, training skills to criterion). The model used in Oklahoma contained three modules: a child health care module designed to help parents prevent illness, recognize when a child is ill, and choose whether to self-treat, call a doctor, or seek emergency care; a home safety module designed to identify and eliminate hazards present in the home and promote home cleanliness; and a parent–child interaction module designed to increase parental bonding with children.

In Oklahoma, the effectiveness of the SC model in reducing out-of-home placements was experimentally tested by implementing the model in three of six regions statewide, while the other three regions continued to provide customary case-management services as usual (SAU). Embedded within this RCT effectiveness trial was a mixed-methods study designed to identify factors that impede or facilitate the implementation of SC, examine the impact of implementation on organizations and staff, and examine the effect of organizational factors on working alliance and client outcomes. Quantitative data were collected using 10 waves of web-based surveys with 21 teams participating in the statewide trial. Qualitative data were collected by means of individual semistructured interviews with clinical case managers, supervisors, and agency directors, as well as focus groups with each of the 21 teams over four waves.

Two of the quantitative studies published to date have identified the impacts of evidence-based practice implementation on the culture and climate of the agencies participating in the effectiveness trial. In the first study, Aarons and colleagues examined the impact of implementation with and without the use of a monitor who observed the use of the SafeCare modules and provided feedback to home visitors (Aarons, Sommerfeld, Hecht, Silovsky, & Chaffin, 2009a). In the study, 21 teams consisting of 153 home-based service providers were followed over a 29-month period, contributing a total of 2,293 observation-months and 57 instances of employee turnover for an overall turnover rate of 0.298 per observation-year ([57 events/2,293 observation-months] × 12 months) or the equivalent of 29.8 turnover events for every 100 person-years observed. Turnover rates (per 100 person-years) for each of the four experimental conditions were as follows: monitored SC = 14.9%, nonmonitored SC = 33.4%, nonmonitored SAU = 37.6%, and monitored SAU = 41.5%. These effects were significant even when controlling for effects of perceived job autonomy, turnover intentions, and work attitudes. Job tenure and work attitudes did not significantly predict turnover. A review of organization theory led to the hypothesis that decreasing job autonomy through the implementation of a more structured approach to services delivery and fidelity monitoring—common characteristics of EBP—would lead to higher turnover intentions and poor staff retention. However, implementation and fidelity monitoring contributed to greater, not less, staff retention.

In the second quantitative study, Aarons and colleagues examined the impact of evidence-based practice implementation and fidelity monitoring on staff emotional exhaustion (Aarons, Fettes, Flores, & Sommerfeld, 2009b). In keeping with the previous study, the investigators hypothesized that providers implementing SafeCare with monitoring would have the lowest levels of emotional exhaustion and those receiving additional monitoring not in the context of implementation would have higher levels of emotional exhaustion relative to the other groups. Results supported the hypotheses in that lower levels of emotional exhaustion were observed for staff implementing the practice but higher levels of emotional exhaustion were observed for staff receiving only fidelity monitoring and providing SAU. Together, these results suggested a potential staff and organization benefit to implementation. In addition, higher provider caseload and younger age were associated with higher levels of emotional exhaustion.

The investigators also examined the impact of organizational culture and climate on the implementation of SafeCare itself in two qualitative studies published to date. In the first study, Aarons and Palinkas (2007) analyzed data collected from semistructured interviews with 15 case managers and 2 ongoing consultants. Case manager participants were selected by maximum variation sampling to represent those having the most positive and those having the most negative views of SafeCare based on results of a web-based quantitative survey asking about the perceived value and usefulness of the evidence-based practice. Six primary factors emerged as determinants of implementation in this study: (1) acceptability of the practice to the caseworker and the family, (2) fit of the practice with the needs of the family, (3) caseworker motivations for using the practice, (4) experiences with being trained in the practice, (5) extent of organizational support for implementation, and (6) impact of the practice on process and outcome of case management.

In a second qualitative study, Palinkas and Aarons (2009) examined agency and program administrator perspectives on factors that facilitated or impeded implementation of evidence-based practices. Grounded theory analytic methods were used to elicit themes from transcripts in semistructured interviews with 13 executive and program directors of agencies participating in the SafeCare effectiveness trial in Oklahoma. The researchers identified six critical determinants of implementation:

1. Availability of resources, including funding, ongoing training, and supervision, and reliance on other agencies for feedback and support
2. Positive external relations with state agencies funding the program and with researchers who give the highest priority to the community partner's goal of providing high-quality and effective services to families and children, are willing to accommodate to the needs and constraints of community partners, are supportive of community partners, and participate in problem solving to implement the evidence-based practice

3. Agency leadership support for evidence-based practices, motivated by monetary gains from having a state contract, the prestige and intellectual gains associated with being part of a research project, the perceived "goodness of fit" between the objectives of SafeCare and the values embedded in the agency's organizational culture, and the potential of using participation in the effectiveness trial and associated training in an evidence-based practice as a marketing tool in recruiting new staff

4. Achieving high motivation/low resistance in staff through the exercise of leadership, deliberate screening, and selection of staff members most open to innovation to participate in the program, use of staff attrition and turnover to weed out staff members resistant to innovation, and providing resources and material support

5. Tangible benefits for staff, including acquisition of new skills and the availability of additional clinical supervision

6. Perceived benefits outweighing perceived costs. Perceived benefits included improved outcomes and quality of care, staff supervision and skill enhancement, client education, and a reinforcement of organizational culture. The perceived costs included an increased workload for staff, additional staffing, additional and unanticipated expenses to support EBP activities, lower morale of staff members who were resistant to change (e.g., those with low dispositional innovativeness or in some cases those with longer job tenure), inconvenience of use of SC with certain families, and the perception that it does not help all families.

Challenges to Conducting Organization-Level Research

The research reviewed in this chapter points to two conclusions. The first conclusion is that research translation is influenced by the organizational context. Values and beliefs held by an organization and its members can facilitate or impede the effectiveness, dissemination, or implementation of an evidence-based practice. An organization with poor psychological climate or workplace attitudes may be less likely to use an evidence-based practice. Even when favorably disposed toward innovation, an organization may wish to adapt the practice to suit its own needs and preferences or the needs and preferences of the clients it serves.

The second conclusion is that organizations are influenced by research translation. Values and operating procedures change as members of an organization become exposed to and obtain firsthand experience with an evidence-based practice. Success with one innovation may foster openness toward other innovations; alternatively, negative experiences with an innovation may make organizations reluctant to consider other innovations. Adoption of new practices and improved performance in the aftermath of such adoption may improve individual morale and organizational climate.

Combined, the two conclusions pose a challenge for conducting translational research at the organization level because they suggest that research translation is a moving target. If the process of translation is affected by its context and the context changes with the process of research translation, then understanding the relationship between translation and context requires methods that take into account the fact that neither will remain static for long.

Related to the challenge of identifying the relevant organizational characteristics at the relevant point in time is the challenge of determining which level or unit of analysis is appropriate for particular implementation outcomes. As Proctor and colleagues (2010) observe, "Certain outcomes, such as acceptability, may be most appropriate for individual level analysis (for example, providers, consumers), while others, such as penetration may be more appropriate for aggregate analysis, at the level of the health care organization." Furthermore, aggregation of individual- or group-level measures to characterize organizations must comply with the theory linking these levels together. For instance, Chan (1998) distinguishes between the direct consensus composition model and the additive composition model in measuring organization-level characteristics. The direct consensus model uses within-group consensus of the individual-level measure as the functional relationship to specify how the construct conceptualized and operationalized at the individual level is functionally isomorphic to another form of the construct at the organizational level. The typical operational combination process is using within-group agreement of scores to index consensus at the lower level and to justify aggregation of lower-level scores to represent scores at the higher level (Chan, 1998, p. 237). The additive model assigns a value to the organization-level measure based on the average of the individual members of the organization. According to Chan (1998, p. 236), in additive composition models, the variance of the lower-level units is of no theoretical or operational concern for composing the lower-level construct to the higher-level construct. The validity of the additive index (e.g., the mean) constitutes empirical support for the composition.

Infrastructure Requirements

Requirements for conducting organization-level translational research are similar in most respects to requirements for conducting translational research at all levels of translation as described in the previous chapter. These requirements include staffing, development of community–academic partnerships, and compensation for study participation. Staffing for the execution of translational research at the organizational level must pay special attention to the multidisciplinary expertise of the research team. Most organization-level translational research has been conducted by investigators trained in business, management, and industrial/organizational psychology. Research on organizations and innovative practices has also been conducted by economists, political scientists, sociologists, anthropologists, and social and clinical psychologists, as well as social workers. The diversity of perspectives is essential to understanding social service agencies as organizations and as social contexts for evidence-based practice translation and implementation. It is at this level that translational research has benefited from the greatest degree of cross-fertilization of theories to explain the reciprocal relationships between organizational factors and research translation and to design strategies to promote research translation through development of receptive organizational structures and processes.

Beyond the diversity of research discipline, a diversity of experience-based perspectives on the role of organizations in translational research is required. As Proctor and colleagues (2009) advise, implementation research requires a partnership of treatment developers, service-system researchers, and quality-improvement researchers. The effectiveness, implementation, and sustainability of evidence-based practices would undoubtedly benefit from a better understanding on the part of treatment developers of the organizational context in which evidence-based practices are used. Such an understanding might be achieved through interactions with experts in implementing quality improvement strategies that seek to improve service through implementation of changes within organizations.

Staffing for the conduct of translational research must also consider the diversity of methods used in understanding and influencing research translation. As noted in this chapter, translational research on organizational factors uses both quantitative and qualitative methods in observational and experimental designs. Since the focus of such research is the organization, sophisticated quantitative methods such as hierarchical linear models are required to address smaller sample size and the nesting of effects within organizations and groups within organizations. Development of new tools for measuring changes in organizations related to translation and implementation of evidence-based practices also calls for expertise in instrument development and psychometric evaluation.

Additional Resources

For additional information on measuring groups and organizations:

Academy of Management Journal
Academy of Management Review
Administration in Social Work

Glisson, C., & James, L. R. (2002). The cross-level effects of culture and climate in human service teams. *Journal of Organizational Behavior*, *23*(6), 767–794. doi:10.1002/job.162

Journal of Applied Psychology

Kimberly, J., & Cook, J. M. (2008). Organizational measurement and the implementation of innovations in mental health services. *Administration and Policy in Mental Health and Mental Health Services Research*, *35*(1–2), 11–20. doi: 10.1007/s10488-007-0143-x

Rousseau, D. (1990). Assessing organizational culture: The case for multiple methods. In B. Schneider (Ed.), *Organizational climate and culture* (pp. 153–92). San Francisco, CA: Jossey-Bass.

6

Mixed-Methods Research

The case studies and much of the research reviewed in the previous two chapters represent a particular approach to conducting research known as mixed methods—the subject of this chapter. Mixed-methods research refers to the integrated use of quantitative and qualitative methods in the same study or project. Although mixed-methods designs have been used in a wide variety of studies, they are considered to be particularly appropriate for conducting translational and implementation research for reasons that are presented in this chapter.

Principles and Practice of Mixed Methods

What Are Mixed Methods?

Several different definitions of *mixed-methods research* exist. Teddlie and Tashakkori (2003, p. 11) define it as a type of research design in which qualitative and quantitative approaches are used in defining the type of questions asked, data collection and analysis procedures used, and/or inferences drawn from the data. Cresswell and colleagues define it as involving "the collection and analysis of both quantitative and qualitative data in a single study in which the data are collected concurrently or sequentially, are given a priority, and involve integration of the data at one or more stages in the process of research" (Cresswell, Plano Clark, Gutmann, & Hanson, 2003, p. 212). Morse denotes the use of mixed methods as occurring "when strategies derived from qualitative and quantitative methods are used in a single project" (2003, p. 191). We use the term *mixed methods* here to refer to the collection, analysis, and integration of both quantitative and qualitative data in a single study or series of studies. It includes both the use of qualitative and quantitative methods within a single paradigm and integration of both quantitative and qualitative paradigms and methods within a single study or project. As Cresswell and Plano Clark (2007) note, it is not sufficient that each type of data be collected and analyzed, but the data must be integrated or "mixed" in some way to form a more complete picture of the problem and its solution.

Why Use Mixed Methods?

Perhaps the best reason for using mixed methods is that quantitative and qualitative approaches used in tandem provide a better understanding of research problems than either approach alone (Cresswell & Plano Clark, 2007). Although mixed-methods designs have been used in several different areas of scholarly inquiry, they have been identified as being particularly relevant to translational and implementation research. Mendel and colleagues (2008) suggest that a mixed qualitative and quantitative approach may be usefully applied within three areas of evaluation of evidence-based practices translation—process, outcomes, and context—and proves especially valuable in linking these types of assessments. Proctor and colleagues (2009) identify mixed methods as being particularly critical in the design and evaluation of strategies designed to facilitate the uptake or implementation of evidence-based practices, interventions and treatments. Wells and colleagues note that community-based participatory research projects include an evaluation of the process of developing the partnership and the intervention, the costs of running the program, and the effect of the program itself on the outcomes of individual participants (Wells, Miranda, Bruce, Alegria, & Wallerstein, 2004). The process evaluation is generally conducted using qualitative methods, while a mixed-methods design is used to evaluate the impact of implementation. Nastasi and Hitchcock (2009) argue that mixed-methods designs are critical to understanding intervention effects within and across layers of multilevel interventions, explaining outcome variations across contexts, and potentially promoting sustainability. Petrucci and Quinlan

(2007) point to mixed methods as a response to the gap between research and practice in social work.

The use of mixed methods in translational and implementation research is also consistent with the call by funding agencies (National Institute of Mental Health, 2004) and others (Proctor et al., 2009) to develop new conceptual models and to develop new measures to test those models. Several studies have focused on the development of new measures (Blasinsky, Goldman, & Unützer, 2006; Slade et al., 2008) or conceptual frameworks (Zazzali et al., 2008) or the development of new interventions or adaptation of existing interventions (Barrio & Yamada, 2010; Henke, Chou, Chanin, Zides, & Scholle, 2008; Proctor et al., 2007). Qualitative methods have been suggested as essential tools for the development of valid and reliable quantitative measures (Patton, 2001) and for the development of conceptual frameworks using an inductive approach to data collection and analysis (Morse, 2003). Social workers have applied mixed-methods techniques for developing such conceptual models, as in the case of Petrucci and Quinlan (2007), who used concept mapping—a mixed-methods strategy that captures rich conceptual data from communities of interest on a particular question and organizes and analyzes it statistically using multidimensional scaling and cluster analysis (Trochim, 1989)—to delineate a theory of therapeutic jurisprudence by developing a framework of validated key components that can form the basis of a standardized instrument.

Mixed methods are also consistent with the need to conduct implementation research in collaboration with potential consumers of evidence-based practices (both practitioners and clients) (Proctor et al., 2009). As observed by Aarons and colleagues (2011), some models that describe approaches to organizational change and innovation adoption highlight the importance of actively including and involving critical relevant stakeholders during the process of considering and preparing for innovation adoption. The use of qualitative methods gives voice to these stakeholders (Sofaer, 1999) and allows partners an opportunity to express their own perspectives, values, and opinions (Palinkas et al., 2009). Obtaining such a perspective was an explicit aim of studies by Henke and colleagues (2008), Proctor and colleagues (2007), and Palinkas and Aarons (2009).

Mixed-methods designs are also viewed as a potential response to the issue of small sample size characteristic of implementation research (Landsverk et al., 2011; Proctor et al., 2009). For example, implementers are often "nested" in organizational units such as a program or team. Qualitative methods can be used to validate the findings of quantitative analyses lacking sufficient power to test certain hypotheses through convergence or triangulation—an explicit feature of the mixed-methods study of the implementation of SafeCare in Oklahoma by Aarons and colleagues examined in the previous chapter. Mixed methods can also be used to provide answers to questions raised by quantitative analyses that quantitative data alone are unable to accomplish (Aarons & Palinkas, 2007; Palinkas & Aarons, 2009).

How Are Mixed Methods Structured?

Numerous typologies and guidelines exist for the adoption of mixed-methods designs. Tashakkori and Teddlie (2003) identified 40 types of mixed-methods designs in their review of the literature, and Cresswell and Plano Clark (2007) highlighted 12 typologies. These typologies represent mixed-methods research in the fields of nursing (Morse, 1991; Sandelowski, 2000), evaluation (Greene, Caracelli, & Graham, 1989; Patton, 2001), public health (Morgan, 1998; Steckler, McLeroy, Goodman, Bird, & McCormick, 1992), primary care (Cresswell, Fetters, & Ivankova, 2004), education (Cresswell, 1999), and the social and behavioral sciences (Cresswell & Plano Clark, 2007; Waszak & Sines, 2003). Most of these typologies of mixed methods include a description of the structure of use by using a taxonomy developed by Morse (1991) that emphasizes the timing—using methods in sequence is represented by a "→" symbol, while using them simultaneously is represented by a "+" symbol—and weighting—the primary method is capitalized while the secondary method is represented in lowercase letters—of each component.

Sequential designs. The first of the sequential designs in translational and implementation research is one in which the collection and analysis of qualitative data take priority and precede the use of quantitative methods (QUAL → quan). Many of these designs involve the quantification of qualitative data. For instance, Proctor et al. created frequencies and rankings of problem categories from a sample of 49 community long-term care clients with a history of depression (Proctor, Hascke, Morrow-Howell, Shumway, & Snell, 2008). These categories were then compared with quantitative measures of depression status obtained through administration of the nine-item Patient Health Questionnaire (Wittkampf et al., 2007). This design is used when the theoretical drive is inductive in nature and commonly used to first develop and then conduct a pilot test of a model or an intervention.

The second sequential design also begins with the use of qualitative methods. However, in this instance, the qualitative methods are secondary to the successive use of quantitative methods (qual → QUAN). For instance, Proctor and colleagues (2007) conducted a qualitative pilot study to capture the perspective of agency directors on the challenge of implementing evidence-based practices in community mental health agencies prior to the development and testing of a specific implementation intervention in the belief that incorporation of this perspective in the development stage would lead to a more successful outcome that would be assessed using quantitative methods. This design is used when the theoretical drive is deductive in nature and commonly used to modify a conceptual framework or adapt an existing intervention before conducting a full test of the model or intervention.

The third sequential design reverses the order and the priority of the two methods such that quantitative methods are used initially but are treated as secondary to the collection and analysis of qualitative methods (quan → QUAL). For instance, a qualitative study of case manager experiences with SafeCare, described in Chapter 5, selected participants for semistructured interviews on the basis of quantitative data obtained from a web-based survey (Aarons & Palinkas, 2007). This design is used when the theoretical drive is inductive in nature and is commonly used to identify a sample of individuals using quantitative methods for a more in-depth investigation of a phenomenon using qualitative methods.

The fourth sequential design also involves the collection and analysis of quantitative data prior to qualitative data; however, the priority of each method is reversed (QUAN → qual). For instance, Sajatovic and colleagues (2005) conducted a qualitative study of patient attitudes toward a collaborative care model of a group psychotherapy intervention for bipolar disorder subsequent to a clinical trial of the intervention. Although the primary objective of the clinical trial was to evaluate the effectiveness of the intervention, the objective of the qualitative study was to identify patient perspectives on the essential ingredients for an effective client–provider relationship and requirements for treatment adherence based on their experience in the trial. This design is used when the theoretical drive is deductive in nature and commonly used when the quantitative study results are unexpected and a qualitative study is helpful in examining the factors that caused the unexpected data (Morse, 2003).

Simultaneous designs. As described by Morse (2003), there are two simultaneous designs, both of which are used in translational and implementation research. The first design gives priority to the collection and analysis of quantitative data (QUAN + qual). For instance, a qualitative-methods assessment of the role of staff turnover in evidence-based practice implementation by Woltmann and colleagues (2008) was conducted as part of a larger project that quantitatively evaluated the effectiveness of an agency- and clinician-level intervention designed to facilitate implementation of five evidence-based practices. This design is used when the theoretical drive is deductive in nature and commonly used to develop a conceptual model or intervention and then test it quantitatively or to examine study components that may not be quantifiable or require explanation or illustration (Morse, 2003).

The second simultaneous design gives priority to the qualitative approach (QUAL + quan). For instance, Bachmann and colleagues (2009) coupled qualitative data from semistructured interviews for the primary purpose of describing and comparing the experience of integrating children's services in children's trusts in England with quantitative data from two cross-sectional questionnaire surveys for the secondary purpose of describing representation on children's and young people's services boards and services most often commissioned jointly. This design is used when the theoretical drive is inductive in nature, and typically used when some portion of a phenomenon may be measured and this measurement enhances the qualitative description or interpretation (Morse, 2003).

Although Morse (2003) argues that one method must inevitably take priority over the other, there are studies in which the priority of a method is not specified (QUAL + QUAN). For instance, Gioia and Dziadosz (2008) used semistructured interview and focus group methods to obtain firsthand accounts of practitioner experiences in being trained to use an evidence-based practice and a quantitative measure of attitudes toward the use of such practices to identify changes in attitudes over time. Neither of these aims was assigned priority over the other, and each aim required a specific method. Similarly, Aarons and Palinkas (Aarons & Palinkas, 2007; Palinkas & Aarons, 2009), simultaneously collected qualitative data through annual interviews and focus groups and quantitative data through semiannual web-based surveys to assess the implementation of SafeCare. The study also assessed its impact on agency organizational culture and climate, as well as the therapeutic relationship between home visitor and client family (QUAN + QUAL).

What Is the Purpose of Mixing Methods?

There are five distinct functions of mixing methods in translational and implementation research: convergence, complementarity, expansion, development, and sampling.

Convergence. This function of mixed methods involves the sequential or simultaneous use of qualitative and quantitative methods to answer the same question. There are two specific forms of convergence—triangulation and transformation (Palinkas et al., 2011). Triangulation involves the use of one type of data to validate or confirm conclusions reached from analysis of the other type of data. For instance, Moffatt and colleagues used a mixed-methods design to evaluate whether welfare rights advice had an impact on health and social outcomes in older adults. Although analysis of the quantitative data suggested no impact of the intervention, analysis of the qualitative data collected from a subsample of participants suggested wide-ranging impacts (Moffatt, White, Mackintosh, & Howell, 2006). Transformation involves the sequential quantification of qualitative data or the use of qualitative techniques to transform quantitative data. For instance, using the technique of concept mapping (Trochim, 1989), Aarons and colleagues solicited information on factors likely to impact implementation of evidence-based practices in public sector mental health settings from 31 services providers and consumers organized into six focus groups (Aarons, Wells, Zagursky, Fettes, & Palinkas, 2009). Each participant then sorted a series of 105 statements and rated each statement according to importance and changeability. Data were then entered in a software program that uses multidimensional scaling and hierarchical cluster analysis to generate a visual display of how statements clustered across all participants. Finally, 22 of the original 31 participants assigned meaning to and identified an appropriate name for each of the clusters identified. Transformation usually occurs sequentially while triangulation typically is based on a simultaneous structure.

Complementarity. Whether used simultaneously or in sequence, the complementary use of quantitative and qualitative methods is used to answer related questions for the purpose of evaluation or elaboration. In evaluative designs, quantitative data are used to evaluate outcomes while qualitative data are used to evaluate process. In elaborative designs, qualitative methods are used to provide depth of understanding and quantitative methods are used to provide breadth of understanding. This includes studies that presented descriptive quantitative data on subjects, and studies that used qualitative data to focus on beliefs and perspectives (Palinkas et al., 2011). For instance, Hoagwood and colleagues (2007) used a case study of an individual child to describe the process of implementation of an evidence-based, trauma-focused, cognitive-behavioral therapy for treatment of symptoms of PTSD in children living in New York City in the aftermath of the World Trade Center attack on September 11, 2001. Although the article included information on the outcome of the child's treatment, the case-study method was intended more to illustrate the process of treatment, beginning with engagement and moving to assessment, treatment, and finally, to outcome. This technique also illustrates the use of an elaborative design in which qualitative methods are used to provide depth of understanding to complement the breadth of understanding afforded by quantitative methods. In this instance, the "thick description" of the child's progress from symptom presentation to completion of treatment offers a degree of understanding of the child's experience, as well as that of other study participants, that is not possible from measures on standardized clinical assessment instruments alone.

Expansion. A third function of integrating qualitative and quantitative methods is expansion, in which one method, usually qualitative, is used in sequence to answer questions raised by the other method, usually quantitative (QUAN ← qual). For instance, Stern and colleagues (Stern, Alaggia, Watson, & Morton, 2008) used standardized instruments and systematic protocols for coding observations to create quantitative measures of therapist adherence to the Incredible Years Parenting Program intervention (Webster-Stratton, Reid, & Stoolmiller, 2008), and qualitative data obtained from audiotapes of supervisory meetings, ongoing supervisory notes, open-ended narrative comments on a survey instrument, and detailed fidelity notes on the intervention process to explain variations in implementation fidelity and identify barriers and facilitators of fidelity.

Development. A fourth function of mixed methods is development in which one method is used to answer questions that will enable use of the other method to answer other questions. There are three distinct forms of development in translational research: instrument development, conceptual development, and intervention development or adaptation. Instrument development involves the sequential use of qualitative data to identify form and content of items to be used in a quantitative study—e.g., survey questions (qual → QUAN). Conceptual development involves the sequential use of qualitative data to create a conceptual framework for generating hypotheses to be tested using quantitative methods (qual → QUAN or QUAL → quan). Intervention development or adaptation involves the sequential use of qualitative data to develop new interventions or adapt existing interventions to new populations (qual → QUAN). In one study (Blasinsky et al., 2006), development of a rating scale to construct predictors of program outcomes and sustainability of a collaborative care intervention to assist older adults suffering from major depression or dysthymia involved the sequential use of qualitative data to identify form and content of items to be used in a quantitative study, such as survey questions (qual → QUAN). In a second study, qualitative data was sequentially collected and analyzed to develop a conceptual framework for generating hypotheses—namely, explaining the adoption and implementation of Functional Family Therapy (Alexander & Sexton, 2002) in a sample of family and child mental health services organizations in New York State—to be tested using quantitative methods (qual → QUAN) (Zazzali et al., 2008). In a third study, Barrio and Yamada (2010) used an iterative process in developing a culturally based family intervention for Spanish-speaking Latino families with a relative diagnosed with schizophrenia. The intervention was based on findings from an ethnographic study. Focus groups and in-depth interviews were then used to explore family members' perceived changes in knowledge, attitudes, and behaviors related to participation in the intervention, and to gather ideas regarding the intervention structure, format, content, and process.

Sampling. The final function of mixed methods in translational research is sampling, or the sequential use of one method to identify a sample of participants for use of the other method. Aarons and Palinkas (2007), for example, selected clinical case managers with the most positive and most negative views of an evidence-based practice for extended semistructured interviews based on results of a web-based quantitative survey on the value and usefulness of SafeCare (quan → QUAL). A study of staff turnover during the implementation of evidence-based practices in mental health care by Woltmann and colleagues (2008) used qualitative data obtained through interviews with staff, clinic directors, and consultant trainers to create categories of turnover and designations of positive, negative, and mixed influence of turnover on outcomes. These categories were then quantitatively compared with implementation outcomes via simple tabulations of fidelity and penetration means for each category (qual → QUAN).

What Is the Process for Mixing Methods?

The integration of quantitative and qualitative data occurs in three forms: merging, connecting, and embedding (Cresswell & Plano Clark, 2007). *Merging the data* involves explicitly combining or integrating two data sets through interpretation of the results of the analysis of each data set, transformation of one data type into the other type, or consolidation of the data into new variables. *Connecting the data* occurs when the analysis of one type of data leads to (and thereby connects to) the need for the other type of data (Cresswell & Plano Clark, 2007), such as when quantitative results that require explanation lead to the subsequent collection and analysis of qualitative data, or when qualitative results serve as the foundation for the collection and analysis of quantitative data in randomized controlled trials of evidence-based practices or studies of evidence-based practice implementation. *Embedding the data* occurs when data of one type is embedded within a design of another type. Embedding may be either sequential or simultaneous (Cresswell & Plano Clark, 2007).

The most common form of mixed-methods process in translational research appears to be embedding, in which a qualitative study is embedded within a larger quantitative effectiveness trial or implementation study. Slade and colleagues (2008) nested a qualitative study within a multisite randomized controlled trial of a standardized assessment of mental health problem severity to determine whether the intervention improved agreement on referrals, and to identify professional and organizational barriers to implementation.

Embedded designs are used to achieve all five functions of mixing methods described earlier and may utilize either a simultaneous or sequential structure, although the former is far more common.

Translational studies also utilize the process of connecting the data in which the insights gained from one type of method are connected to a different type of method to answer related questions through complementarity, expansion, development, or sampling. Thus, the qualitative assessment of agency director perspectives on implementation of evidence-based practices by Proctor and colleagues (2007) was designed as a pilot-stage step in a research agenda to develop and quantitatively test an implementation intervention. Zazzali and colleagues (2008) connected qualitative data collected from semistructured interviews with 15 program administrators to the development of a conceptual model of implementation of Functional Family Therapy that could then be tested using quantitative methods. Another strategy was to build upon the insights gained from one type of study when conducting a second study using a different type of method. For instance, Frueh and colleagues conducted focus groups to obtain information on the target population, their providers, and state-funded mental health systems that would enable the researchers to further adapt and improve a CBT-based intervention for treatment of PTSD before implementation (Frueh, Cusack, Grubaugh, Sauvageot, & Wells, 2006).

Merging is also used in translational research in the analysis phase either to answer the same question through convergence or to address related questions through complementarity. Bachmann and colleagues (2009) merged qualitative data collected from semistructured interviews with quantitative data collected from two surveys to describe and compare the experience of integrating children's services in 35 children's trusts in England. Both sets of data were used to describe the organizational structure, joint planning and commissioning, service delivery and professional roles, and effectiveness and efficiency of services of these trusts.

However, in many mixed-methods studies, more than one process is evident. For instance, Proctor and colleagues (2008) connected data by generating frequencies and rankings of qualitative data on perceptions of competing psychosocial problems collected from a community sample of 49 clients with a history of depression. Researchers then merged the data with quantitative measures of depression status to explore the relationship of depression severity to problem categories and ranks.

Common Designs

Although it is possible to utilize several different strategies for combining different structures, functions, and processes for mixing methods, there appear to be two general patterns of utilizing the various forms of mixed-methods research in developing and translating evidence-based interventions into routine practice. In the practice development design model, investigators use qualitative methods to develop or adapt a specific intervention or conceptual model and then assess its feasibility and acceptability before testing the intervention using quantitative methods. In this model, the qualitative method is connected to the quantitative method. In the RCT/implementation research model, qualitative methods are usually embedded within a larger quantitative study to achieve complementarity, convergence, or expansion.

Case Study

The Child System and Treatment Enhancement Projects (Child STEPs) initiative was launched in 2003 by the Research Network on Youth Mental Health and funded by the John D. and Catherine T. MacArthur Foundation to help bridge the science–practice gap in children's mental health services. As part of this initiative, the Clinic Treatment Project (CTP) examined the implementation and outcomes of two ways social workers can use three evidence-based protocols to treat children aged 8 to 13 for problems involving depression, anxiety, and disruptive conduct. For treatment of anxiety, the specific manualized program was *Coping Cat*, developed by

Kendall (1990). For treatment of depression, the specific manual-ized program was *Primary and Secondary Control Enhancement Training (PASCET)*, developed by Weisz and colleagues (Weisz, Thurber, Sweeney, Proffitt, & LeGagnoux, 1997). For treatment of conduct problems, the specific manualized program was *Defiant Children: A Clinician's Manual for Assessment and Parent Training*, developed by Barkley (1997). These evidence-based treatments (EBTs) were tested in two forms: standard manual treatment, using full treatment manuals, in the forms that have been tested in previ-ous efficacy trials; and modular manual treatment, in which thera-pists learn all the component practices of the evidence-based treatments but individualize the use of the components for each child, guided by a clinical algorithm (Chorpita, Daleiden, & Weisz, 2005). The modular approach to implementing EBTs was examined for four reasons: (1) children rarely present with a single disorder but rather exhibit comorbid conditions; (2) children do not stay put; problems shift during episode of care and new conditions may emerge as others are effectively managed; (3) clinicians often express a dislike for the rigidity and single focus or manualized treatments, making them difficult to sustain in practice; and (4) a modular approach reflects what social workers actually do with EBTs in prac-tice while providing a structure and logic for decision making.

Agencies in Honolulu (n = 4) and Boston (n = 6), as well as 117 therapists (social workers, clinical psychologists, marriage and family therapists) and 173 children, participated in the project. Therapists within the same clinic who consented to participate were randomly assigned to provide treatment for children recruited into the study using either standard or modular manualized treat-ment approaches or their usual approach to clinical care. Therapists randomized to standard manual treatment or modular manual treatment received training in the specific treatment procedures, in addition to weekly case consultation with project supervisors famil-iar with the protocols to assist the clinicians in applying the treat-ment procedures. The children and families who consented to participate in the study were randomly assigned to receive one of the two treatment approaches or usual care.

The Clinic Treatment Project provides an illustration of a mixed-methods design in which quantitative and qualitative methods are used in the same study. Quantitative methods were used to evaluate the effectiveness of the two evidence-based treatment approaches relative to the control (i.e., treatment as usual) condition. Outcomes included changes in individual youth problems and disorders using standardized instruments such as the Brief Problem Checklist (BPC) (Chorpita et al., 2010), Top Problems Assessment (TPA) (Weisz et al., 2011), and Children's Interview for Psychiatric Syndromes–Child and Parent Forms (ChIPS, P-ChIPS), (Weller, Weller, Rooney, & Fristad, 1999a, 1999b). Further, all children were monitored throughout the study through weekly telephone assessments by blinded callers. This information was used to construct a computerized behavioral health reporting system used to assess both child and therapist progress during the course of treatment (Chorpita, Bernstein, Daleiden, & the Research Network on Youth Mental Health, 2008).

During the course of the randomized controlled trial, qualitative methods were used to examine the process and context of implementation of both the standard and modular manualized versions of the three EBTs. Participant observation occurred at meetings of the research network, attendance at training workshops, visits to study clinics, and social events with project clinicians. Approximately 230 hours of observations between January 2004 and March 2007 provided an opportunity to obtain information on study progress and process. These observations represented the 9 months prior to therapist training, 12 months prior to youth enrollment in treatment, and 26 months of active treatment, thus providing a window into the preimplementation and early implementation experiences of therapists.

Extended semistructured interviews with six clinical supervisors—all postdoctoral students used by the CTP—were conducted in September and October 2006. These interviews were conducted with the use of an interview guide that collected information on therapist understanding of the principles and procedures of the standard and modular manual treatments, therapist experience in using the treatments, supervisor experience in supervising and interacting with project therapists to date, and indicators of the acceptance of the treatments by therapists. The interviews were sufficiently open-ended to enable participants to discuss issues they considered to be relevant to implementation. Consistent with the iterative nature of qualitative research (Denzin, 1978), the content of the guide was modified over time as preliminary analyses of initial interviews suggested new directions of inquiry or the need for more detailed information on particular topics. All interviews lasted approximately 1 hour. Brief semistructured interviews were also conducted with 17 therapists and 2 clinic directors in Boston and 7 therapists and 2 clinic directors in Honolulu. All of these therapists were in the standard or modular manual treatment conditions. These interviews were used to collect information on experiences in using evidence-based treatments to date, initial assessments of usefulness and practicality of standard and modular manual treatments, and motivations for participating in the project.

In 2009, a series of follow-up semistructured interviews and focus groups were conducted with 35 therapists from all three treatment conditions, eight clinic/program directors, and three CTP clinical supervisors to assess therapist understanding of, attitudes toward, and experience with the interventions; characteristics of the clinic/program organizational culture and climate; characteristics of the dissemination process (i.e., training and supervision); and likelihood of continuing to use the EBTs as trained upon conclusion of the CTP. Clinic/program directors were also asked if anyone at clinic took the lead role in implementing the EBTs, whether their implementation required any changes in existing clinic policies and procedures, and whether there were any existing external supports and constraints for sustaining these interventions. Focus groups of therapists and clinical supervisors were used to as a "member checking" tool to validate and expand upon preliminary analyses of the semistructured interview data obtained from clinicians.

All data were analyzed using a methodology rooted in grounded theory (Glaser & Strauss, 1967). These procedures are described in detail in Chapter 4. The technique of constant comparison was used to further condense the categories derived from the coding process into broad themes that were then linked together into a heuristic framework by identifying instances in texts where themes were found to "co-occur" (i.e., different codes assigned to the same or adjacent passages in the texts).

The integration of quantitative and qualitative methods in the CTP was based on three components of a taxonomy described by Cresswell and Plano Clark (2007): convergence or triangulation of findings to determine whether different methods provide the same answers to the same question; complementarity of findings to determine whether different methods provide related answers to related questions; and expansion of findings to determine whether one method (in this case, qualitative) can provide answers to questions raised by use of the other method (in this case, quantitative).

The qualitative study was intended to complement the quantitative study by focusing on dissemination and implementation process as the quantitative study focused on effectiveness outcomes. A study by Palinkas and colleagues (2008) identified eight general themes that revealed a heuristic model of implementation of evidence-based treatments for child mental health (Figure 6.1). The eight themes, in turn, were placed into three different categories: (1) long-term implementation intentions, (2) determinants of implementation, and (3) short-term implementation. Three patterns of clinician intentions were relevant to long-term treatment implementation: (1) application with fidelity, (2) abandonment, and (3) selective or partial application. These patterns were perceived to be associated with three pre-implementation factors: (1) lag time between training and use, (2) clinician engagement with the project, and (3) clinician–treatment fit. Four additional factors were both proximal outcomes of the three determinants and "first steps" of implementation: (1) clinician first impressions of the evidence-based treatments after initial use, (2) competence in treatment use, (3) clinician and researcher adaptability, and (4) clinician–researcher interactions.

The qualitative study was also structured to achieve complementarity by examining in depth certain issues that were being

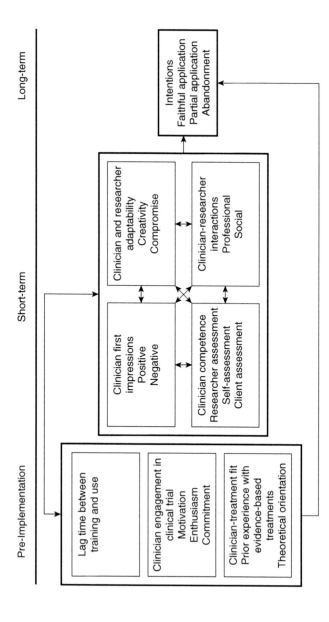

FIGURE 6.1 *Model of Implementation of Evidence-Based Treatment in Randomized Controlled Effectiveness Trials*

(*Source:* Palinkas et al., 2008.)

examined in breadth (i.e., generalizable) in the quantitative study. One particular subject for such an in-depth examination pertained to the interactions between the researchers who developed the treatments and the therapists being trained and supervised in their use. A qualitative study by Palinkas et al. (2009) found that formal and informal interactions between EBT propagators and end users provided access to resources (training in an evidence-based treatment in return for access to study participants) and exchange of global and local knowledge of service delivery (i.e., the EBTs and understanding of client needs and circumstances, respectively). Productive interactions were found to require accessibility, mutual respect, a shared language, and a willingness to engage in negotiation and compromise to resolve differences in demands imposed by organizational culture, the need for EBT fidelity, and the characteristics and specific needs of the clients served by the clinic.

Another question addressed with both quantitative and qualitative data through the function of convergence was whether training in the standard or modular manualized treatment produced any changes in attitudes toward use of evidence-based treatments. An analysis of responses to the EBPAS and Modified Practice Attitudes Scale (MPAS) questionnaires administered before and after training in the two approaches found that therapists' attitudes became significantly more favorable in the modular condition compared to the standard condition, but only on the attitude measure that did not refer specifically to the use of manuals (Borntrager, Chorpita, Higa-McMillan, & Weisz, 2009). These findings suggested that therapists did not harbor negative attitudes toward evidence-based practices as a whole; rather their concerns were with the use of manuals (Borntrager et al., 2009). A similar observation was reported in a qualitative analysis of data collected in the early phases of project implementation with therapists in both conditions reporting that they were likely to use the practices as trained, but in a selective fashion (i.e., use the entire protocol with some clients or some of the protocol with all clients) consistent with the modular approach (Palinkas et al., 2008). During the qualitative interviews, therapists also expressed their concerns over the possible lack of control over the therapeutic process. However, most therapists appeared to have changed their opinions about evidence-based practices once they began using them. For instance, "several clinicians interviewed after training expressed surprise at how well they had been able to use the manuals or how well parents had been engaged in treatment" (Palinkas et al., 2008, p. 743).

Furthermore, the qualitative data helped to expand the findings of the quantitative analysis by explaining why the modular condition was associated with significantly greater change in attitudes. Therapists reported during interviews that the modular condition gave them greater flexibility to pick modules and techniques based on unique needs of client and it did not interfere with their attempts to establish a therapeutic alliance with the client (Palinkas et al., 2008). Both therapists and supervisors thought that the modular approach gave them more "license" to negotiate/exchange with one another (Palinkas et al., 2009).

Challenges in Using Mixed Methods

Interdisciplinary Collaboration

Although mixed methods have come to play an increasingly prominent role in translational and implementation research, they also present a unique set of challenges. Mixed-methods studies are often conducted by an interdisciplinary team of investigators who have specialized areas of expertise, including expertise in quantitative or qualitative methods. Often, mixed-methods studies assume the form of "parallel play" in which investigators conduct separate investigations of the same or related phenomena with very little attempt at integrating these efforts or their results. Mixed-methods designs are deliberately structured to maximize the benefits of each set of methods. Independent engagement of quantitative and qualitative research, even within the context of the same research project, does not constitute mixed methods per se. However, the desire to maximize publication (why write one article describing both quantitative and qualitative findings when they can be divided into two articles?) and the difficulties in collaborating with other researchers who possess different languages, priorities, and perspectives (Robins et al., 2008) tend to promote parallel play rather than integration.

Matching Methods with Study Aims

Another challenge lies in the appropriate matching of method with research aim or objective. Quantitative and qualitative methods are each dependent upon a set of assumptions that help define the circumstances for which either or both methods are necessary and appropriate. For instance, unlike a quantitative study in which data analysis rarely occurs until all data are collected, qualitative research is more iterative in nature; data analysis begins to occur soon after data collection is initiated, allowing for the possibility of revising questions to be asked or methods to be used. While quantitative methods tend to be labeled as objective (separating the researcher from the object of research), scientific (valid, reliable, reproducible, accurate, systematic), general (looking for law-like regularities), technical (procedural, mechanical), and standardized (measurable, verifiable), qualitative methods tend to be labeled as subjective (emerging from the researcher), intuitive (relying upon experiential insight), particular (emphasizing the personal or the context), existential (concerned with everyday experience), and interpretative (related to meaning) (Crabtree & Miller, 1992).

Selection of Appropriate Design

Teddlie and Tashakkori (2003) and Morse (2003) also note two additional challenges involved in using mixed methods. The first challenge relates to the design of mixed-methods studies. Numerous typologies and guidelines for the adoption of mixed-methods designs exist. These typologies represent mixed-methods research in several different fields, as noted earlier, and reflect differences in terminology and nomenclature for similar structural or functional arrangements of quantitative and qualitative components of the same study or qualitative and quantitative studies of the same project. This adds a level of difficulty to communicating and understanding research objectives, constraints, and products. Moreover, there remain few established guidelines for the use of specific design strategies (Robins et al., 2008). For instance, Teddlie and Tashakkori (2003, p. 34) note the controversy surrounding the use of mixed methods for the purposes of triangulation, complementarity, and expansion as types of design or as outcomes of research.

The difficulty in determining whether both methods have equal weight or one carries greater weight based on the theoretical drive parallels the lack of consensus in the literature. Although Morse (2003) argues that a project cannot be informed equally by inductive and deductive studies, Cresswell and Plano Clark (2007) suggest that quantitative and qualitative methods may be given equal weight so that both play an equally important role in addressing the research question. This equal weighting has also been reported in mixed-methods studies in the field of psychology (Waszak & Sines, 2003), and perhaps reflects an effort as well as an opportunity to maximize the qualitative contribution in mental health services research as recommended by Robins and colleagues (2008).

Inference Quality

Another challenge or set of challenges identified by Teddlie and Tashakkori (2003, pp. 38–42) relate to the issue of inferences made when using mixed methods. They note the confusion between quality of data/observations and quality of inferences made by analysis of such data, and recommend that inference quality should be evaluated apart from data quality since the standards for evaluating them are not the same (Tashakkori & Teddlie, 1998). A second challenge with regard to inference is the controversies regarding standards of evaluating inference quality. They suggest four dimensions for evaluating inference quality: within-design consistency, conceptual consistency, interpretative agreement, and interpretive distinctness. The third challenge relates to creating bridges or superordinate standards for evaluating the quality of inferences in mixed-methods research. They recommend four strategies for creating such standards: (1) identify terms that are the same or similar in both traditions; (2) borrow terms from the qualitative orientation that have potential to represent concepts in both; (3) borrow terms from the quantitative orientation that have potential to represent concepts in both; and (4) construct totally new terms (Teddlie & Tashakkori, 2003, p. 42).

Infrastructure Requirements

Staffing

As with the other methods for conducting translational research, mixed methods is inherently interdisciplinary and requires staff with expertise in quantitative and/or qualitative methods. However, there are no clear guidelines for selection and management of such individuals. Teddlie and Tashakkori (2003, p. 44) identified three current models for professional competency and collaboration relevant to the staffing of mixed-methods studies. In the first model, a single investigator uses methods from both traditions. Such a model addresses the challenges associated with different languages and perspectives. However, it is very rare for a single individual to be equally proficient in qualitative and quantitative methods, and conducting research in isolation from other investigators tends to minimize the benefits of collaboration and exchange of different viewpoints and perspectives. Morse (2003) and others have deliberately discouraged this approach, arguing that it is virtually impossible to maintain fidelity to the differing assumptions inherent in each set of methods.

The second model is to adopt a team approach to conducting mixed-methods research with a division of responsibility for collecting and analyzing quantitative and qualitative data. This approach maximizes the expertise in both sets of methods without the necessity of additional training, and avoids the problems associated with mixing of methods described by Morse (2003). However, this model is also more likely to produce parallel play rather than true integration of methods, thereby eliminating the advantages associated with integrated use of both types of methods.

A third and perhaps the most preferred model is to establish and maintain a minimum level of competency in both quantitative and qualitative designs on the part of all researchers in the project, together with a highly specialized set of competencies in one of the two designs. Although the application of such designs operate best when adopted by a team of investigators, each having expertise in quantitative or qualitative methods, all investigators should possess a minimum competency in both sets of methods (Newman & Benz, 1998), as well as the development of a common language for team members to understand one another (Teddlie & Tashakkori, 2003).

Financing

A second infrastructure consideration for conducting mixed-methods studies is the prioritizing of study components when resources are finite, as they inevitably are. Qualitative methods are often incorrectly assumed to be relatively inexpensive to conduct because they usually involve smaller samples of participants and because the methods are perceived to lack the rigor of quantitative methods. However, qualitative methods can be quite labor intensive. The time required to collect the data, transcribe any electronically recorded interviews or focus groups (which can take up to 4 hours for every 1 hour of recorded material), and then systematically code and analyze the data can, on occasion, make the cost of engaging in qualitative research prohibitive. When combined with the time and resources necessary to conduct a quantitative component, the infrastructure requirements for conducting a mixed-methods study may exceed the resources available. In the event this occurs, one can prioritize the components based on the theoretical drive of the study (inductive or deductive) and the timing of the data collection and analysis activities (simultaneous or sequential).

Additional Resources

For additional information on mixed methods:

Cresswell, J. W., & Plano Clark, V. L. (2007). *Designing and conducting mixed methods research*. Thousand Oaks, CA: Sage.

Journal of Mixed Methods Research

Tashakkori, A., & Teddlie, C. (Eds.). (2003). *Handbook of mixed methods in social and behavioral research*. Thousand Oaks, CA: Sage.

For additional information on mixed methods in implementation research:

Palinkas, L. A., Aarons, G. A., Horwitz, S. M., Chamberlain, P., Hurlburt, M., & Landsverk, J. (2011). Mixed method designs in implementation research. *Administration and Policy in Mental Health and Mental Health Services Research*, *38*(1), 44–53. doi: 10.1007/s10488–010-0314-z

7

Community-Based Participatory Research

The objective of this chapter is to discuss the use of community-based participatory research (CBPR) methods in conducting research on the effectiveness, dissemination, and implementation of evidence-based practices. Although CBPR has been widely used in public health to conduct needs assessments or develop community-specific disease prevention and health promotion interventions, these methods are fundamental to translational research because research translation cannot possibly occur without community participation. In essence, communities constitute natural laboratories for translational research. The failure of many practices and interventions to move from research to translation has often been explained by the community's perception that the practices either lack relevance to their specific needs or deprive them of the ability to control the process of service delivery, on the one hand and to contribute to research and translation, on the other. Moreover, these methods are consistent with core social work values of promoting social justice and social change with and on behalf of clients, including communities, and promoting the responsiveness of communities to individual needs and social problems.

Principles and Practice of Research

Fundamental to any form of translation from one language to another are elements of communication, collaboration, and compromise. Communication lies at the heart of all translation, but a translator (i.e., sender) can never know whether the effort to translate is successful unless some response is elicited from the audience (i.e., receiver) that conveys an acknowledgment that the translation (i.e., message) is understood. Both the sender and receiver must act in a collaborative fashion. However, the act of translation is often imperfect as many terms found in one language do not have an exact parallel in another language. Hence, some compromise between sender and receiver is required to construct a meaning of the translated term that both may agree upon.

The elements of communication, collaboration, and compromise are also critical to the translation of research into practice, and constitute the foundation of CBPR. CBPR is not a research method per se but rather a "collaborative approach to research that equitably involves all partners in the research process and recognizes the unique strengths that each brings. CBPR begins with a research topic of importance to the community with the aim of combining knowledge with action and achieving social change to improve health outcomes and eliminate health disparities" (Minkler & Wallerstein, 2003, p. 4). Collaborators communicate with one another for the purpose of generating and sharing knowledge to improve the functioning of community organizations and the health and well-being of community members (Currie et al., 2005). The balance between these two goals is achieved through negotiation (Macaulay et al., 1999).

Initially developed to promote international and rural development, CBPR has been widely used in the field of public health (Israel, Eng, Schulz, & Parker, 2005; Israel, Schulz, Parker, & Becker, 1998; Wells, Staunton, Norris, & the CHIC Council, 2006) to identify risks and suggest solutions to issues as diverse as HIV/AIDS, domestic violence and sexual assault, cancer, diabetes, mental health, and workplace health. This research has led to a growing recognition of its importance and potential by health services organizations, public health institutions, and funding organizations. National policy directives and research initiatives from federal agencies such as the National Institutes of Health, Agency for Healthcare Research and Quality, Centers for Disease Control and Prevention, and Institute of Medicine (e.g., IOM, 2001; National Advisory Mental Health Council, 1998, 2000, 2001) have emphasized the need for increased collaboration between researchers and practitioners in facilitating the translation of research into practice that is both relevant to community needs and effective in reducing disparities in access and quality of care. However, CBPR "shares many of the same values of the social work profession, including the development of collaborative partnerships with the community being served, co-constructing a research agenda that privileges all voices in a reciprocal process, addressing health from a strengths-based community perspective, and sharing the implications of the research findings with community members and assisting in the development of innovative solutions" (Jones, Pomeroy, & Sampson, 2009, p. 95).

CBPR differs from other forms of community-based research, much of which either "targets" a community or is conducted within a community with minimal involvement of community members other than serving as research "subjects" (Wells et al., 2004). As Wallerstein and Duran (2006) observe, CBPR is distinguished from other forms of community-based research by its emphasis on developing and managing relationships between university-based researchers and community collaborators and by its focus on achieving social change through community empowerment.

Principles of CBPR

Israel and colleagues (2003) identified four fundamental assumptions that govern the conduct of CBPR: (1) genuine partnerships require a willingness of all stakeholders to learn from one another; (2) in addition to conducting the research, there is commitment to training community members in research; (3) the knowledge and other products gained from research activities should benefit all partners; and (4) CBPR requires a long-term commitment of researchers to the community and of the community to the goal of improving the health and well-being of its members. Based on these assumptions, Minkler and Wallerstein (2003) proposed a set of principles, which are listed in Table 7.1.

Table 7.2 illustrates how CBPR differs from traditional forms of translational or other research. Not described in this table, however,

TABLE 7.1. Principles of Community-Based Participatory Research

1. Recognizes *community* as a unit of identity.
2. *Builds on strengths* and resources within the community.
3. Facilitates a *collaborative, equitable partnership* in all phases of research, involving an empowering and power-sharing process that attends to social inequalities.
4. Promotes *co-learning and capacity building* among all partners.
5. Integrates and achieves a *balance between knowledge generation and intervention* for the mutual benefit of all partners.
6. Focuses on the *local relevance of public health problems* and ecological perspectives that attend to the multiple determinants of health.
7. Involves systems development through a *cyclical and iterative* process.
8. *Disseminates results* to all partners and involves them in the wider dissemination process.
9. Involves a long-term process and commitment to *sustainability*.

Source: Minkler and Wallerstein, 2003.

are the characteristics of CBPR participants. More so than in traditional research, university-based researchers must be willing to communicate, collaborate, and compromise. This means they must be willing to share their knowledge and expertise with community partners and know how to speak with them in a manner that demonstrates respect and uses a language or terminology they understand. Researchers must also recognize that working together for the benefit of the community is their main priority and that they must cooperate in identifying the problem and developing the solution. Most important, they must be willing to seek and consider alternative solutions to the problem and to forgo self-interests for the sake of community interests.

When compared to traditional forms of translational research, CBPR may place additional demands on researchers, including having to share power over the direction of the project and the allocation of resources and having to spend a considerable amount of time building trust in the community. However, CBPR also offers certain benefits compared to traditional translational research, including those listed in the following box.

- Helps the community meet its needs met through research that is actually relevant
- Helps the research and academic community conduct more valid, quality research with respect to the community
- Helps to bridge gaps in understanding, trust, and knowledge between academic institutions and the community
- Achieves higher-quality and more useful results by taking into account the full context of individuals, rather than seeing people in isolation from their environment, culture, or identity
- Provides empowerment of and equal control by people who historically have had little say in the research performed upon them or about them (Autistic Spectrum Partnership in Research and Education, 2010; Israel et al., 1998)

TABLE 7.2. Comparison of Characteristics of Traditional Research with Characteristics of Community-Based Participatory Research

	Traditional Research	Community-Based Participatory Research
Goal of research	Advance knowledge	Betterment of community
Source of research question	Theoretical work	Community-identified problem
Designer of research	Trained researcher	Trained researcher and community
Role of researcher	Outside expert	Collaborator, learner
Role of community	Subject of study	Collaborator, learner
Relationship of researcher to participants	Short-term, task-oriented, detached	Long-term, multifaceted, connected

TABLE 7.2. (*Contd.*)

	Traditional Research	*Community-Based Participatory Research*
Value of research	Acceptance by peers (e.g., publications)	Contributions to community change
Ownership of data	Academic researcher	Community
Means of dissemination	Academic conferences, journals	Any and all forums, media, meetings, community

Source: Strand, Marullo, Cutforth, Stoecker, and Donohue, 2003.

Practice of CBPR

As illustrated in Figure 7.1, CBPR projects involve a sequence of activities related to project development, implementation, and dissemination. Project development includes identifying a health or social welfare issue that fits community priorities and academic capacity to respond to the issue. This may require an assessment of community needs, resources, and definition of the issue and the identification of a strategy to address the issue (Israel et al., 2005). Project development also requires the development of a coalition of community, policy, and academic stakeholders that informs, supports, shares, and uses the products, as well as engaging the community through conferences and workshops that provide information, determine readiness to proceed, and obtain input (Jones & Wells, 2007). Project implementation includes creation of work groups that develop, implement, and evaluate action plans under a leadership council (Jones & Wells, 2007) and documentation and evaluation of implementation processes and outcomes (Israel et al., 2005). Project dissemination includes interpreting project process and outcomes, obtaining feedback from all collaborators, and communicating and applying results (Israel et al., 2005).

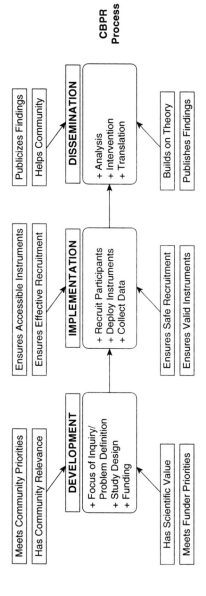

FIGURE 7.1 *Community-Based Participatory Research Process*

(*Source:* Academic Autistic Spectrum Partnership in Research and Education, 2010.)

Models of Research–Practice Partnerships

For the most part, research–practice partnerships exist along a continuum of models, with investigator-initiated research and minimal community input at one end and joint decision making on all aspects of research with active community direction and interpretation of the results at the other end (Baker, Homan, Schonhoff, & Kreuter, 1999; Hatch, Moss, Saran, Presley-Cantrell, & Mallory, 1993). Most of these models presume that the quality, effectiveness, and sustainability of interventions implemented and evaluated in community settings improve as one moves along this continuum. The models, in turn, govern the specific activities of the partners. For instance, using the principles of CBPR and cultural exchange theory, a partnership between an academic research center and a large public mental health system was developed with the goal of improving care for middle-aged and older people with schizophrenia and other psychoses (Lindamer et al., 2008). Development and maintenance of the partnership involved the following phases: (1) building and sustaining the partnership; (2) mobilizing community support and enhancing infrastructure for community research capacity; (3) generating knowledge (research and training); (4) transferring knowledge to community practice (dissemination and implementation); and (5) evaluating outcomes and process. Public participation in each of these phases ensured clinical and cultural relevance to communities and contributed to the effectiveness and sustainability of the interventions, programs, and practices that resulted from such research.

One of the best-known models of translational research–practice partnerships is the evidence-based community/partnership model developed by Ken Wells and colleagues at UCLA and RAND. "This model is designed to support health improvement goals through evidence-based strategies while building community and practice capacity to implement those strategies in a manner consistent with community priorities, culture, and values. This model relies on a partnership between communities, community advocates, health care practices, and researchers, blending techniques of community participatory intervention and evidence-based quality improvement programs" (Wells et al., 2004, p. 958). The model is implemented in two steps: (1) development of a negotiated set of goals among local community stakeholders, practices, and researchers and (2) matching community needs, resources, and values with EBP strategies tailored to address unmet needs and community context. "This may involve adapting practice interventions for local community practices and developing complementary community interventions to extend the reach of practice interventions into the community. It may also include building capacity in the practices to increase the engagement and retention of economically disadvantaged clients to benefit from evidence-based care or building the capacity of community agencies to assess practice interventions" (Wells et al., 2004, p. 958).

CBPR and Social Work Translational Research

There are several examples of social work translational research that are based on CBPR models and principles. They include Safe at Home, an intimate partner violence prevention project (Begun, Berger, Otto-Salaj, & Rose, 2010); Heart to Heart, an HIV risk–reduction project for women with alcohol or substance abuse problems (Begun et al., 2010), and the promotion of translational research on evidence-based practices in aging by the Cornell Institute for Translational Research on Aging (CITRA) (Wethington et al., 2007). A good illustration of the application of CBPR principles in social work translational research is the Chicago HIV Prevention and Adolescent Mental Health Project (CHAMP). CHAMP was developed in response to the increasing need to both understand and intervene in exposure to HIV risk factors among urban youth. The project sought to understand sexual development and HIV risk in context and apply that understanding to the development of an intervention program—the CHAMP Family Program. The CHAMP Family Program's content and structure were influenced by research conducted in the communities targeted for intervention and the application of a collaborative model in creating partnerships of community parents, school staff, and university-based researchers (Madison, McKay, Paikoff, & Bell, 2000).

The CHAMP collaborative model was designed to address obstacles to community-based prevention research arising from insufficient resources, lack of community participation, and tensions between community residents and outside researchers (Dalton, 1989; Thomas & Quinn, 1991). It was understood that research efforts that failed to appreciate local and culturally specific stressors or the community's core values would most likely fail to achieve their long-term objectives, including HIV prevention (Sperber et al., 2008, p. 2). Several different strategies were adopted to facilitate engagement of community members in the research process and to promote collaboration between university-based researchers and the community in achieving research goals and objectives. For instance, focus groups were conducted with community parents and children to identify which factors needed to be studied. Community members were also trained to code videotaped interaction with participating families. The CHAMP Collaborative Board helped to determine the leadership, design, implementation, and evaluation of several projects, including the 12-session CHAMP Family Program (Madison et al., 2000).

The activities of the CHAMP Collaborative Board also help to illustrate five essential tasks considered to be critical to the development and maintenance of this collaboration: (1) development of trust between partners; (2) information exchange; (3) shared decision making; (4) leadership development; and (5) transfer of ownership. According to Madison and colleagues (2000, p. 287), the central issue at the outset of the project was the need of community board members "to feel that the researchers could be trusted to work with the community and that they were credible and honest people." The need to establish a framework for insuring that such trust could be maintained resulted in the creation of a mission statement, which explicitly stated that the research was being conducted *for* the community and not *to* the community. The mission "evolved into a commitment to fully transfer the program (ownership, leadership, and administration) to community members so that the prevention work can continue and expand after research funding has ended" (Madison et al., 2000, p. 288). In turn, the board committed to hiring community residents for positions and patronizing local businesses. All board members were compensated for their participation. The final step in the board's participation in curriculum development occurred when parent board members became pilot participants, allowing them to become intimately familiar with the intervention and preparing them to assume responsibility for its implementation. "This became the critical juncture where board members became versed in the curriculum, as both receivers and future deliverers of the program, and were able to shape the final product" (Madison et al., 2000, p. 289). Board members also helped negotiate the logistics of delivering the program at the school sites.

More recently, McKay and colleagues (2010) have used collaborative strategies to increase engagement of highly vulnerable youth in mental health services. Three programs are currently under evaluation: the Multiple Family Group (MFG), designed to address conduct difficulties among inner-city youth through a family-based and mutual support service delivery model; HOPE, a family-based HIV prevention and mental health promotion program created through collaboration between an urban community collaborative board, a working group of inner-city parents, school staff members, and university-based researchers; and Step-Up, a school-based mental health service delivery model developed to bolster key family and youth processes related to youth mental health and risk-taking behaviors. All three interventions were co-designed, co-delivered, and collaboratively evaluated by academic and community-based partners. Preliminary evidence suggests that all three interventions are associated with significant reductions in youth mental health symptoms (McKay et al., 2010).

CBPR Methods

CBPR has long been associated with a predominantly qualitative approach to data collection and analysis, an approach that extends into the conduct of translational and implementation research in community settings. There are several reasons for this association. First, as Wells and colleagues (2004) observe, the goals and approaches used in participatory community interventions cannot be fully specified in advance due to the need to integrate researcher and community preferences and perspectives. Consequently, evaluations of such interventions rely on action research methods and qualitative or mixed methods because such methods are appropriate for exploratory research (Teddlie & Tashakkori, 2003). Second, "community interventions shift the focus away from individuals and towards the process of engagement and impacts on communities, entailing a different measurement and assessment process" (Wells et al., 2004, p. 957). Unlike other community-based research, CBPR projects include an evaluation of the process of developing both the partnership and the intervention. This evaluation initially focuses on process using qualitative methods and later focuses on outcomes using both quantitative and qualitative methods. Third, community preferences and priorities for service delivery often limit the ability to implement research with randomized or quasi-experimental designs. Consequently, community interventions are typically evaluated through case study and action research models by using qualitative or mixed methods with a strong focus on intervention process. Finally, CBPR relies primarily on qualitative methods to engage populations served in forming research questions, collecting data, taking action with the knowledge gained, and disseminating information (Healy, 2001; Israel et al., 2003; Jones et al., 2009). These activities reflect paradigms of empowerment and participatory research (Pinto, McKay, & Escobar, 2008).

One such method for engaging community members in collection and analysis of data is a technique developed by anthropologists known as Rapid Assessment Procedures (RAP). This approach is designed to provide depth to the understanding of the event and its community context that is critical to the development and implementation of more quantitative (cross-sectional or longitudinal) approaches involving the use of survey questionnaires and diagnostic instruments (Scrimshaw & Hurtado, 1987). Distinguishing features of RAP include (1) formation of a multidisciplinary research team including a member or members of the affected community; (2) development of materials to train community members; (3) use of several data collection methods (e.g., informal interviews, newspaper accounts, agency reports, statistics) to verify information through triangulation; (4) iterative data collection and analysis to facilitate continuous adjustment of the research question and methods to answer that question; and (5) rapid completion of the project, usually in 4 to 6 weeks (Harris, Jerome, & Fawcett, 1997). Essentially, the methodology is based on techniques of participant observation and nondirected interviewing. Palinkas and colleagues have used RAP to engage community collaborators in studies of community response to school violence (Palinkas, Prussing, Landsverk, & Reznik, 2003; Palinkas, Prussing, Reznik, & Landsverk, 2004) and to assess of mental health service needs of older adults (Barrio et al., 2008; Palinkas et al., 2007).

Another qualitative technique often used in CBPR studies is Photovoice, a method that involves giving cameras to people to take photographs that illustrate issues that concern them. Necheles et al. (2007) used this technique to engage youth in identifying influences on their health behaviors, including unhealthy food choices, inducers of stress, friends, emotions, environment, health, and positive aspects of family. Pile sort techniques were used to separate photographs into discrete, meaningful categories that were expanded upon through multiple group discussions and individual semistructured interviews. Other techniques include use of a qualitative case-study methodology for gathering and interpreting community member stories (Miller & Crabtree, 2005). Letcher and Perlow (2009) used this technique to explore the experiences of participants in a study of social participation and well-being.

Although qualitative methods continue to predominate in CBPR studies, researchers are increasingly using quantitative methods and randomized trial designs. Quantitative methods are also being adopted to assess the impact of the partnership itself. King and colleagues (2009) developed a measure of partnership impact called the Community Impacts of Research Oriented Partnerships (CIROP), a 33-item instrument with excellent internal consistency (Cronbach's alpha coefficients ranging from .92 to .97), acceptable test–retest reliability, and good construct validity.

Case Study

Communities That Care (CTC) (Hawkins & Catalano, 2002; Hawkins, Catalano, & Arthur, 2002) is a community-based strategic approach and manualized prevention service delivery system that mobilizes and empowers communities to adopt an evidence-based framework for the implementation of evidence-based practices to prevent adolescent health and behavior problems. CTC is designed to increase communication, collaboration, commitment, and ownership among community members and service providers (Hawkins et al., 2002; Hawkins, Guo, Hill, Battin-Pearson, & Abbott, 2001). In this respect, CTC represents a form of CBPR. For instance, CTC helps community members collect data on risk and protective factors at the local level. The community is also empowered to choose from a growing number of evidence-based interventions that are suited to the community profile of risk, protection, and demographics. Community leaders establish a shared vision for the future of the community's children; community members are encouraged to support and participate in the efforts to move toward this vision; and local providers, including teachers, human services workers, and community volunteers, implement this vision after completing training in the selected practices (Hawkins et al., 2002, 2008).

The theory of change underlying CTC posits that selection of effective prevention programs and strategies should be tailored to the specific epidemiology of risk and protection found in communities. This is operationalized in communities via repeated epidemiological assessments of adolescent risk and protective factors used for strategic prevention planning and ongoing evaluation of prevention service delivery systems (Arthur & Blitz, 2000). Additionally, social development strategies (Catalano & Hawkins, 1996; Hawkins & Weis, 1985) are incorporated into CTC training activities and technical assistance to provide specific guidelines for implementation

(Fagan, Hawkins, & Catalano, 2008; Quinby et al., 2008). These strategies are designed to develop positive social bonds through involvement in a social group such as a coalition, family, or class, as well as acquisition of social skills and recognition for their contributions to the group (Hawkins, Catalano et al., 2008, p. 179). These bonds, in turn, inhibit the development of problem behaviors in individual youth and the communities in which they reside. By producing greater adoption of evidence-based prevention, increased collaboration among service providers, and increased use of tested and effective preventive interventions that address risk and protective factors prioritized by the community, CTC aims to produce changes in the risk factors targeted by the preventive interventions chosen by the community. These reductions in risk factors in the community are expected, in turn, to reduce adolescent delinquent behaviors and substance use among young people (Hawkins, Brown et al., 2008, pp. 15–16).

The CTC process involves five specific phases:

- *Phase 1:* Key leaders are mobilized to assess their community's readiness to adopt the CTC approach to prevention.
- *Phase 2:* Local residents are appointed to a prevention board by community leaders. Board members receive a series of six training sessions delivered over the course of 6 to 12 months by certified CTC trainers. These training sessions describe the public health model, prevention science, and the advantages of using a data-driven decision-making process to guide prevention activities. All CTC training materials are available on the Internet.
- *Phase 3:* The prevention board uses community-specific epidemiological data to assess levels of risk and protection and conducts a resource assessment of prevention programs already occurring in the community. The board then assesses the epidemiology of problem behaviors in their community, identifies the prevalence of community risk and protective factors associated with these outcomes, and prioritizes which risk and protective factors should be addressed and which outcomes are of most concern.

- *Phase 4:* The prevention board then selects evidence-based prevention programs to address the prioritized risk factors and outcomes from a menu of interventions found to be effective with this age group. Each intervention included in the menu has demonstrated positive effects in reducing one or more risk factors and reducing delinquent behavior or substance use in youths aged 10 to 14. CTC also offers training, technical assistance, and manuals to guide the implementation of the policy or program (Hawkins, Brown et al., 2008, p. 16).

- *Phase 5:* The prevention board supports the implementation of these programs, conducts an ongoing evaluation of their effectiveness in the community, and engages in continuous quality improvement by revising their plans as necessary (Jonkman et al., 2008, p. 44). Evaluation is based on ratings of the CTC Milestones and Benchmarks (Quinby et al., 2008) that are to be achieved during the five phases of CTC system implementation. The milestones are goals to be met by communities, and the benchmarks are the actions that community members take or conditions that must be present to achieve those goals.

The effectiveness and implementation of the CTC program were evaluated in a community-randomized trial known as the Community Youth Development Study (CYDS) (Hawkins, Catalano et al., 2008). This study was conducted in 24 communities across the United States. The CYDS had four distinct aims: (1) to examine the efficacy of the CTC system in affecting levels and trends in risk and protection, and reducing the incidence and prevalence of adolescent substance use and delinquency in students and communities; (2) to assess levels of collaboration among various sectors within communities (e.g., civic, business, youth recreation, religious) as a system-level mediator between program adoption and changes in levels of risk and protection in communities; (3) to examine the use of epidemiological data to prioritize community-specific risk and protective factors and the selection of appropriate and effective prevention programs that address those factors; and (4) to examine whether the use of these selected prevention programs is related to changes in community levels of risk, protection, substance use, and delinquency (Brown et al., 2009, p. 313). Investigators reported significantly lower mean levels of targeted risks for seventh graders in CTC communities compared with controls (Hawkins, Catalano et al., 2008). Significantly fewer students in CTC communities than in control communities initiated delinquent behavior between grades five and seven. A follow-up study (Hawkins et al., 2009) reported the incidences of alcohol use, cigarette and smokeless tobacco initiation, and delinquent behavior were significantly lower in CTC than in control communities for students in grades five through eight. In grade eight, the prevalence of alcohol and smokeless tobacco use during the previous 30 days, binge drinking during the previous 2 weeks, and different delinquent behaviors committed during the previous year was significantly lower for students in CTC communities.

Challenges to Using CBPR

Role Definition

Despite the increasing recognition of the importance of including community participation when conducting translational and implementation research, there are numerous challenges associated with CBPR. One of the primary challenges is defining the roles each stakeholder is to assume in the project. "Protocols that document the roles and functions can be used to support community staff training and increase program reproducibility and reliability. During intervention development and implementation, partnership members may adopt different roles at different project stages; one indicator of a successful partnership may be flexibility in shifting roles to support different goals" (Wells et al., 2004, p. 959).

Differences in Organizational Cultures

Another significant challenge is the existence of competing languages, priorities, and perspectives of researchers and community members.

In essence, researchers and practitioners represent two distinct groups, each with their own values and perspectives. These distinctions have often been viewed as a challenge to collaboration, even when the two groups have shared similar goals and objectives, and have occasionally led to conflicts between researchers and practitioners. For instance, Wells and colleagues (2004) have observed that differences in the priority of practitioners for sustaining interventions versus the priority of researchers for identifying experimental effects and outcomes have led to conflict between the two groups of collaborators. In adapting the CHAMP intervention in Trinidad and Tobago, "investigators found that the competing missions of a direct service agency, community members and researchers [were] a serious challenge. Local stakeholders had difficulty understanding the value of allocating funds for methodical 'study,' when more funds allocated to service provision could help more people" (Sperber et al., 2008, p. 5). Begun and colleagues (2010, p. 58) reported that during a multisite project, "the staff members were highly committed to providing the services and followed the treatment protocol (which they had helped to develop) with great fidelity. However, they were not uniformly committed to data collection (although they had helped design the instruments and procedures) because they did not see an immediate benefit for their clients. As a result, they were unreliable in collecting quality data."

Competing priorities assigned to science versus practice is only one of the differences in the organizational cultures of researchers and practitioners that pose a challenge to conducting community-based translational and implementation research. "The social justice perspective of CPPR means that projects serve community capacity-building priorities. This perspective can be challenging to sustain because academic medicine is competitive while CPPR is inclusive and collaborative" (Jones & Wells, 2007, p. 409). Researchers and practitioners also differ with respect to terminology, agendas, time-tables, interests, and expectations (Allen-Meares, Hudgins, Engberg, & Lessnau, 2005; Begun et al., 2010). The implementation of evidence-based practices itself has been a source of conflict, as researchers have been perceived as advocating for their exclusive use and limiting the definition of evidence to the experience of conducting randomized controlled trials, and practitioners have been perceived as being resistant to such practices and evidence on the grounds that both are not necessarily relevant to "real world" clinical populations and settings, thus minimizing the value of evidence gained from firsthand clinical experience (Begun et al., 2010).

Overcoming Mistrust

Related to these differences in organizational cultures, researchers often face the challenge of overcoming the mistrust of "outsiders" that community members often exhibit. In many instances, this mistrust is the legacy of prior negative experiences community members have had with other researchers. Begun and colleagues (2010, pp. 55–57), for instance, note the following:

> Our community partners relate past unfortunate experiences with university "partners" who had little interaction with them during project conceptualization or development. Others report their experiences with university "experts" who tell them what to do or how they should do things . . . . Similarly, our university partners have sometimes encountered community partners who hold unrealistic research expectations that cannot reasonably be fulfilled (for example, helping prove a cherished position or providing money for services). . . . All too often scientists encounter distrust and suspicion of research from agencies and social workers in practice. Our agency partners have reported several unfortunate experiences with university researchers who conducted "hit and run," "smash and grab," or "parachute" studies. The negative result on the university-agency relationship is that these experiences leave agency partners feeling violated, used, and robbed.

In adapting the CHAMP family intervention in Trinidad and Tobago, investigators encountered suspicion on the part of community members as foreigners—particularly Americans—whom many Trinidadians associate with the negative impact of tourism and media (Sperber et al., 2008, p. 5). Consequently, researchers are required to devote considerable time and effort to gaining the trust of community members before proceeding.

Scientific Rigor

Concerns about the scientific rigor of CBPR also pose a challenge to conducting community-based translational and implementation research (Viswanathan et al., 2004). This concern relates to both the methodology for evaluating the outcome of the intervention and the fidelity with which the intervention is used by community-based practitioners. Biglan and colleagues, for instance, pointed to the tension that exists when moving from treatment efficacy to effectiveness between the relative value of research-based fidelity versus input and program adaptations offered by community members and local service providers (Biglan, Mrazek, Carnine, & Flay, 2003). This tension is also noted by Bierman (2006, p. 91), who states: "Moving from efficacy to effectiveness thus requires attention to local, cultural, and context-relevant adaptations based on the input of school and community partners; yet, adaptations that are too extensive or involve changes in the core intervention model or change strategies run the risk of decreasing fidelity and thereby decreasing impact." Consequently, "community and school-based coalitions may make decisions about intervention programming based upon consensus or local wisdom, in some cases with little regard for existing developmental and clinical research" (Bierman, 2006, p. 92).

Distribution of Funding and Resources

Researchers and community partners must also contend with the inevitable imbalance in distribution of funding and other resources. When adapting the CHAMP intervention in Trinidad and Tobago, U.S.-based investigators were not able to share power completely with community partners because they were obligated by the terms of their federal funding to assume final responsibility for fiscal management and institutional review (Sperber et al., 2008). Moreover, participation and control are never static as research projects may begin with a university-driven agenda but eventually move toward a mutual agenda or a community-driven agenda over time (Wallerstein & Duran, 2006).

Ethical Conduct of Research

Other challenges are related to the ethical conduct of research in community settings. These include implementation of efforts to ensure that informed consent is obtained and the participant confidentiality is protected (Brydon-Miller & Greenwood, 2006). For instance, "the question of who represents the community always remains a challenge, as no community is homogeneous, and community organizations or leaders who invite universities into their communities still may not represent the range of community interests . . ." (Wallerstein & Duran, 2006, p. 315).

Solutions to Challenges

Fortunately, the experience derived from the CBPR projects described in this chapter offers a number of potential solutions to these challenges. It goes without saying that sustained funding is essential to the success and long-term sustainability of any research program. However, its role in CBPR projects is especially crucial as it helps to address the challenges related to lack of resources and potential imbalance of power and control over resources (Greenberg, Feinberg, Gomez, & Osgood, 2005).

Exchange Technology

Begun and colleagues (2010) encourage collaborators to develop a "technology exchange" perspective in conducting CBPR projects. Such a perspective acknowledges the unique contributions of each partner active in the collaboration. For instance, the university-based researcher may contribute the scientific rigor while the community partner may contribute knowledge of the community and practice-based experience necessary to create a community-based program or translate research evidence into effective practice. The researcher may contribute personnel and resources necessary to evaluate the practice's effectiveness, while the community partner may contribute a field site necessary to evaluate the relevance, utility, and cultural validity of the practice (Wong, 2006). However, for such an exchange to take place, the community partner and the research partner must share equally in the risks, the work, and the rewards of their project (Wong, 2006).

Develop a Longitudinal Perspective

A second perspective suggested by Begun and colleagues necessary for overcoming the challenges of engaging in CBPR projects is longitudinal or developmental in nature. This perspective acknowledges that such partnerships take time to develop and that the most time-intensive element is the building of trust among community members. Based on their experience with the CHAMP project, Madison and colleagues (2000) observed that the development of relationships built on trust was critical and could not be rushed. Preparing community board members to play influential roles required a lengthy and gradual process of immersion in the background and content of the intervention program. Based on this experience, they recommend that research projects should plan to devote up to 12 months to developing collaborative relationships before developing key aspects of the research and/or intervention. Wong (2006) recommends taking on smaller projects to identify common interests before initiating major projects. She also cautions researchers to expect numerous ups and downs in community support and program development.

The longitudinal perspective also requires an acknowledgment that, eventually, a shift in the balance of power will occur with the university-based researcher assuming primary responsibility for research design and resource acquisition at the initial stages and the community assuming ownership of the intervention at the end of the project. "An engagement process can build trust, ownership, and therefore commitment to research-based system change and improvement by shifting authority of action to consumers, community members, and community-based agencies most affected by programs . . . " (Mendel et al., 2008, p. 28).

Maintain Openness and Clarity in Transactions

A third lesson learned from past CBPR projects is the need to establish openness and clarity in all transactions. According to Begun and colleagues (2010, p. 56), "achieving clarity concerning financial arrangements, budgets, and contracts is a key process in creating and maintaining long-standing, effective research partnerships." To achieve such clarity, they provided several recommendations, including those given next.

- Collaborative partnerships can be well served by the establishment of clear and unambiguous contracts or formal agreements, including well-developed budgets, in the context of developing clear lines of organization and management (Reid & Vianna, 2001). These types of preemptive agreements may range in complexity from a simple consulting arrangement based on a letter of understanding between an individual and an agency to a full-fledged contract (or subaward contract) between institutions.
- Regardless of agreement type, it is critical to establish who has the legitimate authority to enter into the agreement at both the university and the community partner sites.
- Regardless of the agreement format, university and community partners need to establish a clear statement of the scope of work to be conducted and who is responsible for

which aspects, as well as expected products and timelines for each research activity. Issues of intellectual property rights require exploration and formal agreements as well.

- Other contracting topics to consider include conditions for termination of the partnership, conflict of interest, liability language, licensure, and agency-specific compliance certification or assurances.
- Budgeting and payment details should be agreed on in writing if money is involved in the research partnership (Begun et al., 2010, pp. 60–61).

Learn about Collaborators

A fourth lesson learned is the importance of understanding precisely who the collaborators are, what motivates them to collaborate, and any aspects of their organizational culture that might influence the degree and nature of their collaboration. "Establishing and maintaining a collaboration that can unify participants on the basis of their common interests while addressing each participant's unique concerns about the project is a monumental task" (Allen-Meares et al., 2005, p. 34). "Communication depends not only on being able to develop mutual agendas but also on recognizing differences between academic and community interests, skills, and needs, and on developing willingness and mechanisms to deal with inevitable conflicts that emerge because of these differences. Naming differences and recognizing differential access to resources or power can be a critical first step to developing the trust needed for collaborative work . . . " (Wallerstein & Duran, 2006, p. 320).

Engage in Cultural Exchange

One approach to understanding these differences is to frame the knowledge exchange that occurs between university-based researchers and community practitioners as an exchange of perspectives, both global and local in nature. For the most part, researchers provide a global, evidence-based approach to services found to be effective with other populations in other settings. Community-based practitioners, on the other hand, provide a local knowledge of the specific needs of clients in the research sites as well as experience addressing these needs through long-established treatment strategies (Palinkas et al., 2009). The exchange of knowledge is central to EBP. This global–local distinction shares many similarities to the distinction made by Wallerstein and Duran (2006) between empirically supported interventions (ESIs) and culturally supported interventions (CSIs). They note that relying on ESIs "may inadvertently delegitimize knowledge that comes from the local community. ESIs often have been tested in the dominant culture or in a particular minority community and require translational research to assess the applicability to the new community of interest" (2006, p. 315). CSIs, on the other hand, "or the indigenous theories of etiology, practices, and programs that emerge from communities (Hall, 2001; Miller & Shinn, 2005) have often never been formally evaluated or subject to research rigor, yet they are widespread" (2006, pp. 315–316).

The exchange of global versus local knowledge reflects the challenge as well as the opportunity of translational research. The challenge lies in attempting to integrate very different value orientations. For instance, EBP is often associated with a more positivistic tradition of clinical practice, while the distinctive, individualized practices and perspectives of many of the clinicians in both studies tend to reflect a more postmodernist, social constructivist orientation toward behavior and practice (Robbins, Chatterjee, & Canda, 2006). The perspective of treatment developers is usually oriented toward the desire to advance and apply the science of social work, while the perspective of social work practitioners is oriented primarily toward the desire to advance practice through the application of theory and practices consistent with their prior training and experience. In essence, the challenge faced by both groups is in accommodating different priorities rooted in two different cultural systems (Palinkas et al., 2005), one academic and one clinical.

Both the structure and process of cultural systems are encapsulated in a set of shared understandings or value orientations. Value orientations are complex but definitely patterned, resulting from the traditional interplay of basic values (normative values), social values (prescriptive ethics), and their physical expression (artifacts). These give order and direction to human organization. The cultural logic that articulates the normative values of a social service agency explains why it does what it does, while the social knowledge that is embedded in the prescriptive ethics explains how it is done. The artifacts of the normative and prescriptive values explain what is done, who does it, when it is done, and where it is done. These three elements are arranged in hierarchical fashion with the normative truths at the top and the artifacts at the bottom (Bailey, 1973; Davies et al., 2000; Palinkas et al., 2005). The higher the element, the more resistant it is to change from the outside.

Cultural innovations like evidence-based practices involve the translation, transformation, and exchange of the cognitive (information) and affective (motivation) elements of meaning systems of the stakeholders involved in the community–academic partnership. Cultural exchange is a transaction of knowledge, attitudes, and practices that occurs when two individuals or groups of individuals representing diverse cultural systems (ethnic, professional, organizational, national) interact and engage in a process of debate and compromise (Brekke et al., 2007; Palinkas et al., 2005). It is a bidirectional process in which two or more participants (stakeholders) derive something from and are changed as a result of the transaction. As Jones and Wells (2007, p. 410) note, "participatory research can be transformative." In contrast to other models of community-based research, cultural exchange is both a theory and a method, a means of understanding this transaction as well as a tool for facilitating transactions involving multiple stakeholders.

The application of cultural exchange in translational research is based on the fulfillment of several requirements. First, cultural exchange requires an understanding of the value hierarchies of the partners.

Knowing why the partner is involved in the collaboration is important in predicting how each will participate in developing a collaborative working relationship. One common motivation is the desire to bring improved social work services to a particular population. It is not necessary that everyone have the same motivations, but it is important that disparate motivations be recognized, understood, and respected. Without such acknowledgment, it becomes difficult to design strategies to satisfy as many of the distinct needs or desires as possible (Begun et al., 2010, p. 58).

Second, cultural exchange relies heavily on interpersonal processes that require the development and nurturance of reciprocal perceived trust (Brinkerhoff, 2002; Muthusamy & White, 2005; Vangen & Huxham, 2003). "In participatory research, skills are required in developing trust with community members and leaders and dealing with differences in authority" (Wells et al., 2004, p. 957).

Third, cultural exchange requires a willingness and ability to engage in negotiation and compromise with one's partners. For instance, "researchers' interests in knowledge production are often different from the practical interest of communities in improving programs and services in community settings. These issues are important to negotiate throughout the research endeavor so that communities can directly benefit in shorter time cycles, even if final analysis and publications is a long-term process" (Wallerstein & Duran, 2006, p. 314). In the CHAMP project, both researchers and community members had to exercise a certain degree of compromise to ensure the success of the project, with the former learning to make time and room for the expanded roles of community partners and the latter learning to trust researchers to both listen to their perspectives and be willing to adapt interventions based on what they heard (Madison et al., 2000, p. 295).

Cultural exchange also requires that each partner exercise a degree of cultural humility—"'a lifelong commitment to self-evaluation and self-critique' to redress power imbalances and 'develop and maintain mutually respectful and dynamic partnerships with communities' (Tervalon & Murray-Garcia, 1998, p. 118)" (Wallerstein & Duran, 2006, p. 316).

Finally, cultural exchange may require or benefit from the presence of individuals who possess some familiarity or competence in both cultural systems and can serve in the role of culture broker. As Wong (2006) observes, there are numerous benefits from having "champions" for the research and programs on both sides and at several levels. Community liaisons must play an active role in translating the relevance of the science and the need for rigorous methods to stakeholders at all levels.

Infrastructure Requirements

Staffing

In conducting CBPR, consideration must be given to staffing, communication, and compensation. Two types of training are essential to the development and maintenance of community–research partnerships. Community partners must be trained in the essential elements of research methods, including an overview of the principles and practice of translational research; the techniques of data collection, management, and analysis; and procedures for dissemination of research results. Research partners must be trained in the essential elements of working in communities, including an overview of community priorities and preferences and the context of the study communities that may facilitate or hinder the translation of research into practice. Ideally, both groups would participate in the same training activities to ensure that each is aware of the extent of mutual understanding of the roles and responsibilities of all partners.

For their part, researchers must understand that community research is time-intensive, requiring long-term commitment to particular communities to develop trust among community collaborators. In addition to time, such partnerships require strong social skills and patience. According to Mendel and colleagues (2008,

p. 32), "the time and effort required to build, negotiate, and manage relationships . . . can become increasingly substantial as the level of collaboration with stakeholders in the dissemination and evaluation process increases, leaving participants both 'enriched and overwhelmed' (Bluthenthal et al., 2006)." It requires "interdisciplinary collaborations and training that span public health, health services, community, and policy research; qualitative, quantitative, and mixed methods; and investigator skill in community participatory research and coalition building as well as evidence-based practice interventions" (Wells et al., 2004, p. 960).

Communication

Infrastructure support is also required to facilitate ongoing communication among researchers and community partners. As noted earlier, this includes the creation of community advisory boards that can work with researchers to identify service needs and target populations, communicate community preferences that may impact research design and data collection, assist in participant recruitment and data collection and analysis, disseminate research findings to community residents and policy makers, and identify means to sustain effective practices and programs. Both the roles of each board member and the operation of the board itself must be clearly specified in a contract or memorandum of agreement. Communication is also facilitated through the organization and conduct of community forums in which researchers obtain feedback as to community needs, preferences, and concerns and community residents obtain a clear understanding of research aims, operations, and results.

Compensation

A third infrastructure requirement is that of compensation for individual community members and to community agencies and organizations engaged in research activities. Compensation for individuals may occur in the form of cash payments; however, such payments are often discouraged by institutional review boards on the grounds that such compensation might serve as a form of coercion to participate, especially among economically vulnerable populations. Other forms of compensation such as store vouchers or coupons to purchase items through online shopping networks, are frequently used. Compensation for community agencies is critical to ensure that funds are distributed fairly and appropriately so that community partners are not unduly burdened by their participation or feel exploited by outsiders with little investment in the community. "Academic researchers must not only assist with funding programs on the community side but also help with problems by developing timely evaluations and analyses for the community partner. In turn, the agency partners play a crucial role in being advocates and supporters of the research aspects of the program, facilitating data collection, and actively participating in the interpretation of data and preparing material for publication" (Wong, 2006, p. 152).

Additional Resources

For additional information on CBPR:

Minkler, M., & Wallerstein, N. (Eds.). (2003). *Community-based participatory research for health.* San Francisco, CA: Jossey-Bass.

For additional information on community-partnered participatory research:

Ethnicity and Disease (2006). Issue 16, Suppl. 1.

For additional information on Communities That Care and the Community Youth Development Study:

Hawkins, J. D., Catalano, R. F., & Associates. (1992). *Communities That Care: Action for drug abuse prevention* (1st ed.) San Francisco, CA: Jossey-Bass.

8

Conclusion

Future Directions for Translational and Implementation Research

Introduction

As we noted in the first chapter, our intent was to begin with an overview of the "lay of the land" in terms of the latest in translational research, with a focus on the methods used to assess program or practice effectiveness, dissemination, and implementation. We then examined three components of research translation: process, outcomes, and context. We used the organizational level of practice change as the locus for our examination of research translation. Finally, we highlighted the use of two specific methodological approaches to conducting translational research: mixed methods and community-based participatory research. In this final chapter, we summarize the main themes of the book introduced in each chapter and discuss how these themes are linked together to articulate a strategy for conducting translational research. We conclude with an examination of the future of translational research within the field of social work.

Main Themes

The goal of this book was not to introduce a strategy for translation of research into practice but rather to introduce a strategy for conducting translational research—that is, research on the process of translating research into practice. However, it should be clear by now that translational research is inextricably linked with research translation or evidence-based practice (EBP). Translational research involves an examination of the process of research translation from effectiveness to dissemination and implementation, as highlighted in Figure 1.1. It also involves efforts to facilitate translation, both directly through the design and evaluation of strategies like community development teams, the RE-AIM model, or the ARC intervention model, and indirectly through the production of knowledge or research evidence on the translation process itself. While studying the process of research translation may be viewed as a passive activity, the active influencing of that process through research is more in keeping with the values and aims of the social work profession, which is to effect change.

A second theme of the book relates to the interrelationship between the process, outcomes, and context of research translation. Research translation or EBP is itself a process that presumably should lead to improved service delivery. These improvements can be represented as outcomes that measure organizational performance in terms such as costs and benefits of service delivery, or individual performance in terms such as client/patient/consumer health and well-being. These outcomes tell us whether the innovative practices work as predicted, but they cannot tell us why they do not work, or why they work in one setting with one group of clients and not in another setting or with a different group of clients in the same setting. Most important, they do not tell us why these practices are not routinely used or sustained. To answer these questions, we must examine the process by which researchers evaluate the effectiveness of these practices in real-world settings and disseminate the evidence supporting the likelihood of effective outcomes. It also requires an examination of the process by which practitioners adopt, use, and sustain these practices. Above all, it requires us to examine the setting that serves as the context for research translation, given that not all contexts are alike and features of one context may bode well for the effectiveness, dissemination, and implementation of one innovative practice while the features of another context may not. Translational research, therefore, calls for an integrated focus on evidence-based practice outcomes, process, and context.

Such integration is necessary to both understand the phenomenon of research translation and EBP and influence that phenomenon through research and practice.

A third theme relates to the locus of translation. Although translation may be conceived as occurring on four different levels—external environment, organizational, group, and individual—we elected to focus on the organizational level. Organizations represent the context of research translation and the focal point of translational research. It is here that the interaction between research translation/EBP and translational research occurs. Organizations exist in a wider "outer context" characterized by revenue streams, policy mandates, lawsuits demanding the provision of certain services to certain constituencies, rules and regulations, knowledge generation support systems (i.e., universities, professional organizations, clearinghouses), and consumer demands in the forms of social and psychological problems that need to be addressed and of preference for particular services, including those with a research evidence base. This wider context exerts an influence on the culture and climate of a service organization that, in turn, exerts an influence on the process of research translation, as described in Chapter 5. However, the organization itself constitutes a context for understanding the attitudes and behaviors of teams of service providers and individual practitioners as they struggle with the task of adopting, using, and sustaining innovative practices. As the research profiled in Chapter 5 illustrates, some organizations offer a more favorable context for implementation and sustainment of evidence-based practices or interventions than do others. While a comprehensive understanding of research translation/EBP requires a multilevel approach that encompasses both inner and outer contexts, the organizational level is considered the key to examining and understanding this process.

The final theme relates to methods of translational research. Mixed-methods designs involve the integration of techniques for the collection and analysis of quantitative and qualitative data. The emphasis here is on integration in the belief that greater understanding is achieved when both sets of methods are used in combination.

Similarly, community-based participatory research involves the integration of perspectives and activities of university-based researchers and community-based practitioners. Again, the emphasis is on integration in the belief that greater understanding of the process of research translation is achieved when both groups of stakeholders work together than when they work separately, with researchers usually assigned the role of evaluating the effectiveness of the program or practice and practitioners usually assigned the role of implementing the program or practice. Neither can be achieved without the involvement of the other. However, both methodological approaches require a certain degree of communication, collaboration, and compromise between the individuals and their perspectives.

Communication, collaboration, and compromise constitute the core elements of the process of cultural exchange. We envision cultural exchange as a strategy for engaging in translational research. Whether it is an exchange between researchers representing different academic disciplines or methodological approaches, or an exchange between researchers and practitioners, cultural exchange is as fundamental to research translation as it is to translational research. Cultural exchange is also the mechanism by which translational research becomes *transformative*.

Future Directions

Infrastructure Development

Much of the work profiled in this book describes research that occurred in social work practice settings or involved social and psychological needs. Unfortunately, most of this research was led by investigators who were not social workers. If we are to develop a genuine integration of research and practice, of research translation and translational research, the development of social work leadership in translational research must be given high priority. Social workers need to move from being the object of research to actively conducting the research. Social work researchers and practitioners need to integrate the perspective and values that define the profession into the practice of translational and implementation research. As we observed in Chapter 1, social workers are in a unique position to lead the field of translational research because of their experience in assuming the roles of change agent and culture broker. Translation is all about changing lives, institutions, and society. However, accomplishing such change requires an ability to bring together individuals and organizations representing different values, expectations, and perspectives of the proper course of action. This ability requires that social workers communicate with all stakeholders, collaborate with them in achieving an agreed-upon set of goals and objectives, and be willing to reach a compromise when disagreements arise as to the means or ends of EBP/research translation.

Parallel to the development of social work leadership in translational research is the development of an infrastructure for conducting such research. Priority should be given to instruction in conducting and using systematic reviews and web-based clearinghouses that offer guidance on EBP and the procedures for conducting EBP/translational research. Schools of social work should offer courses on methods for conducting effectiveness, dissemination, and implementation research. The current efforts of the Council on Social Work Education and National Association of Social Workers to promote EBP do not always translate into curriculum development to create the knowledge base necessary for conducting translational research. Social work researchers must exercise leadership in curriculum development as well as study design and execution.

A third area of development relates to the formation and maintenance of collaborative frameworks that are interdisciplinary and multimethod and involve partnerships between university-based researchers and community-based practitioners. Creation of opportunities that enable social workers to learn from and contribute to the work of colleagues from other fields is an essential step to developing a supportive infrastructure for conducting social work translational research. Integration of quantitative and qualitative methods in mixed-methods designs calls for not only interaction with experts in each type of method but an ability to communicate across methodological approaches and develop a common language that facilitates communication and collaboration between such experts. It may also require some degree of compromise between the epistemological foundations and standards of scientific rigor associated with each set of methods. The ability to communicate, collaborate, and compromise is also considered an essential requirement for using community-based participatory research methods when conducting translational research. As noted in the last chapter, this ability usually requires both time and a commitment on the part of researchers and practitioners to acknowledge differences in organizational cultures and priorities based on those cultures. It requires a sense of mutual trust, understanding of each stakeholder's goals and constraints, and support for each stakeholder's contribution to a common goal.

Finally, a supportive translational research infrastructure requires development of "translation laboratories," organizational settings where translational research can be conducted. Such laboratories must be community based and offer a platform for training as well as research on evidence-based practice effectiveness, dissemination, and implementation. Developing such laboratories will require resources, including funding for research and sustainment of evidence-based practices or interventions, personnel, and technology to facilitate communication among stakeholders, as well as data collection and analysis. The community network cores of NIMH-funded Advanced Centers for Innovation in Services and Implementation Research are a potential model for the creation of such community-based translational research laboratories.

Advancing the Field

Finally, we suggest four specific ways that social workers can help to advance the field of translational and implementation research. The first way is to contribute to the development of guidelines for conducting translational research that effect a compromise between the need to respect methodological integrity and the need to accept the realities of conducting research in community settings.

These realities include limitations on controlling for organizational procedures or environmental factors that may confound effectiveness, dissemination, and implementation outcomes and accommodation of the priorities and limited research skills of community partners. As noted in Chapter 4, researchers must be willing to face the reality that the randomized controlled trial may not always be preferable, much less possible, when engaged in translational research in community-based settings. Advancing the field of translational research may require experimentation with alternatives to the traditional randomized controlled trial design.

A second opportunity for social workers to advance the field of translational research lies in developing guidelines for the use of mixed methods. As noted in Chapter 6, there exist several different taxonomies describing the combination of quantitative and qualitative methods with origins in disciplines like education, public health, sociology, psychology, and evaluation. The diversity of taxonomies and the guidance they offer in conducting mixed-methods research begs the question of whether there is an agreed-upon way of correctly using such methods. Consensus needs to be established to make such a determination, and the familiarity of social work researchers with both quantitative and qualitative methods suggests they are well positioned to establish such consensus.

A third opportunity to advance the field lies in developing strategies for monitoring or measuring change when the context of that change, whether it is the organization or the external environment, is itself changing and being changed by the translation process. Advances in longitudinal mixed-effects models that incorporate time as a level of analysis offer one possible way of tracking changes in outcomes and context over time.

Finally, we propose that social work researchers advance the field of translational research by developing strategies for moving between translational research and research translation. In the past, researchers have endeavored to create a wall between efforts to study the process of research translation and efforts to influence that process through their research. The concern was that combining the two sets of activities would compromise validity and introduce bias into collection and analysis of translational research data. However, if the two activities are fundamentally linked, as we have argued, then researchers and practitioners must develop strategies and methodologies for determining which of the two activities one happens to be operating at a single point in time. If it turns out, as we suggest, that one is always engaged in both activities simultaneously, then standards for identifying bias and sources of measurement error associated with this simultaneous engagement must be established and technologies for adhering to these standards must be developed.

In conclusion, it is our belief that translational research offers an important opportunity for social workers. No academic discipline can survive without innovation, and innovation is the foundation of social work practice. Translational research and research translation both require collaboration, communication, and compromise between researchers and practitioners; neither can occur without the participation of both communities.

References

Aarons, G. A. (2004). Mental health provider attitudes toward adoption of evidence-based practice: The Evidence-Based Practice Attitude Scale (EBPAS). *Mental Health Services Research, 6*(2), 61–74. doi:10.1023/B:MHSR.0000024351.12294.65

Aarons, G. A. (2006). Transformational and transactional leadership: Association with attitudes toward evidence-based practice. *Psychiatric Services, 57*(8), 1162–1169. doi:10.1176/appi.ps.57.8.1162

Aarons, G. A., Cafri, G., Lugo, L., & Sawitzky, A. (2010). Expanding the domains of attitudes towards evidence-based practice: The Evidence Based Practice Attitude Scale-50. *Administration and Policy in Mental Health and Mental Health Services Research.* doi:10.1007/s10488–010–0302–3

Aarons, G. A., Fettes, D. L., Flores, L. E., Jr., & Sommerfeld, D. H. (2009). Evidence-based practice implementation and staff emotional exhaustion in children's services. *Behaviour Research and Therapy, 47*(11), 954–960. doi:10.1016/j.brat.2009.07.006

Aarons, G. A., Hurlburt, M., & Horwitz, S. M. (2011). Advancing a conceptual model of evidence-based practice implementation in public service sectors. *Administration and Policy in Mental Health and Mental Health Services Research, 38*(1), 4–23. doi: 10.1007/s10488-010-0327-7

Aarons, G. A., & Palinkas, L. A. (2007). Implementation of evidence-based practice in child welfare: Service provider perspectives. *Administration and Policy in Mental Health and Mental Health Services Research, 34*(4), 411–419. doi:10.1007/s10488–007–0121–3

Aarons, G. A., & Sawitzky, A. C. (2006). Organizational culture and climate and mental health provider attitudes toward evidence-based practices. *Psychological Services, 3*(1), 61–72. doi:10.1037/1541-1559.3.1.61

Aarons, G. A., Sommerfeld, D. H., Hecht, D. B., Silovsky, J. F., & Chaffin, M. J. (2009). The impact of evidence-based practice implementation and fidelity monitoring on staff turnover: Evidence for a protective effect. *Journal of Consulting and Clinical Psychology, 77*(2), 270–280. doi:10.1037/a0013223

Aarons, G. A., Wells, R. S., Zagursky, K., Fettes, D. L., & Palinkas, L. A. (2009). Implementing evidence-based practice in community mental health agencies: A multiple stakeholder analysis. *American Journal of Public Health, 99*(11), 2087–2095. doi:10.2105/AJPH.2009.161711

Academic Autistic Spectrum Partnership in Research and Education. (2010). Community based participatory research. http://aaspire-project.org/about/cbpr.html

Achenbach, T. M. (1991). *Manual for the Child Behavior Checklist/4–18 and 1991 profile*. Burlington: University of Vermont, Department of Psychiatry.

Alexander, J. F., & Sexton, T. L. (2002). Family functional therapy: A model for treating high risk, acting-out youth. In F. W. Kaslow & J. L. Lebow (Eds.), *Comprehensive handbook of psychotherapy: Vol. 4, Integrative/eclectic* (pp. 111–132). New York, NY: John Wiley & Sons.

Allen-Meares, P., Hudgins, C. A., Engberg, M. E., & Lessnau, B. (2005). Using a collaboratory model to translate social work research into practice and policy. *Research on Social Work Practice, 15*(1), 29–40. doi:10.1177/1049731504272345

Amodeo, M., Ellis, M. A., & Samet, J. H. (2006). Introducing evidence-based practices into substance abuse treatment using organization development methods. *American Journal of Drug and Alcohol Abuse, 32*(4), 555–560. doi:10.1080/00952990600920250

Anderson, N. R., & West, M. A. (1998). Measuring climate for work group innovation: Development and validation of the Team Climate Inventory. *Journal of Organizational Behavior, 19*(3), 235–258. doi:10.1002/(SICI)1099-1379(199805)19:3<235::AID-JOB837>3.0.CO;2-C

Arthur, M. W., & Blitz, C. (2000). Bridging the gap between science and practice in drug abuse prevention through needs assessment and strategic community planning. *Journal of Community Psychology*, *28*(3), 241–255. doi:10.1002/(SICI)1520-6629(200005)28:3<241:: AID-JCOP2>3.0.CO;2-X

Atkins, M. S., Frazier, S. L., Leathers, S. J., Graczyk, P. A., Talbott, E., Jakobsons, L., . . . & Bell, C. C. (2008). Teacher key opinion leaders and mental health consultation in low-income urban schools. *Journal of Consulting and Clinical Psychology*, *76*(5), 905–908. doi:10.1037/a0013036

Bachmann, M. O., O'Brien, M., Husbands, C., Shreeve, A., Jones, N., Watson, J., . . . & the National Evaluation of Children's Trusts Team. (2009). Integrating children's services in England: National evaluation of children's trusts. *Child: Care, Health and Development*, *35*(2), 257–265. doi:10.1111/j.1365-2214.2008.00928.x

Bailey, F. G. (1973). Promethian fire: Right and wrong. In F. G. Bailey (Ed.), *Debate and compromise: The politics of innovation* (pp. 1–15). Totowa, NJ: Rowman & Littlefield.

Baker, E. A., Homan, S., Schonhoff, R., & Kreuter, M. (1999). Principles of practice for academic/practice/community research partnerships. *American Journal of Preventive Medicine*, *16*(3), 86–93. doi:10.1016/S0749-3797(98)00149-4

Bandura, A. (1986). *Social foundations of thought and action: A social cognitive theory*. Englewood Cliffs, NJ: Prentice Hall.

Barkley, R. A. (1997). *Defiant children: A clinician's manual for assessment and parent training* (2nd ed.). New York, NY: Guilford Press.

Barrio, C., Palinkas, L. A., Yamada, A.-M., Fuentes, D., Criado, V., Garcia, P., & Jeste, D. V. (2008). Unmet needs for mental health services for Latino older adults: Perspectives from consumers, family members, advocates, and service providers. *Community Mental Health Journal*, *44*(1), 57–74. doi:10.1007/s10597-007-9112-9

Barrio, C., & Yamada, A.-M. (2010). Culturally based intervention development: The case of Latino families dealing with schizophrenia. *Research on Social Work Practice*, *20*(5), 483–492. doi:10.1177/1049731510361613

Barwick, M. A., Peters, J., & Boydell, K. (2009). Getting to uptake: Do communities of practice support the implementation of evidence-based practice? *Journal of the Canadian Academy of Child and Adolescent Psychiatry*, *18*(1), 16–29.

Begun, A. L., Berger, L. K., Otto-Salaj, L. L., & Rose, S. J. (2010). Developing effective social work university–community research collaborations. *Social Work*, *55*(1), 54–62.

Bierman, K. L. (2006). Commentary on the pitfalls and pratfalls of evaluation research with intervention and prevention programs. *New Directions for Evaluation, 110*, 87–96. doi:10.1002/ev.189

Biglan, A., Mrazek, P. J., Carnine, D., & Flay, B. R. (2003). The integration of research and practice in the prevention of youth problem behaviors. *American Psychologist, 58*(6–7), 433–440.

Blasinsky, M., Goldman, H. H., & Unützer, J. (2006). Project IMPACT: A report on barriers and facilitators to sustainability. *Administration and Policy in Mental Health and Mental Health Services Research, 33*(6), 718–729. doi:10.1007/s10488–006–0086–7

Bluthenthal, R. N., Jones, L., Fackler-Lowrie, N., Ellison, M., Booker, T., Jones, F., . . . & Wells, K. B. (2006). Witness for Wellness: Preliminary findings from a community–academic participatory research mental health initiative. *Ethnicity and Disease, 16*(1, Suppl. 1), S18–S34.

Borgatti, S. P, Everett M. G., & Freeman, L. C. (2002). *Ucinet for Windows: Software for Social Network Analysis*. Harvard, MA: Analytic Technologies.

Borntrager, C. F., Chorpita, B. F., Higa-McMillan, C., & Weisz, J. R. (2009). Provider attitudes towards evidence-based practices: Are the concerns with the evidence or with the manuals? *Psychiatric Services, 60*(5), 677–681. doi:10.1176/appi.ps.60.5.677

Boruch, R. (2007). Encouraging the flight of error: Ethical standards, evidence standards and randomized trials. *New Directions for Evaluation, 2007*(113), 55–73. doi:10.1002/ev.215

Brekke, J. S., Ell, K., & Palinkas, L. A. (2007). Translational science at the National Institute of Mental Health: Can social work take its rightful place? *Research on Social Work Practice, 17*(1), 123–133. doi:10.1177/1049731506293693

Breslow, N. E., & Clayton, D. G. (1993). Approximate inference in generalized linear mixed models. *Journal of the American Statistical Association, 88*(421), 9–25. doi:10.2307/2290687

Brinkerhoff, J. M. (2002). Assessing and improving partnership relationships and outcomes: A proposed framework. *Evaluation and Program Planning, 25*(3), 215–231. doi:10.1016/S0149–7189(02)00017–4

Bronfenbrenner, U. (1979). *The ecology of human development: Experiments by design and nature*. Cambridge, MA: Harvard University Press.

Brouwers, E. P. M., De Bruijne, M. C., Terluin, B., Tiemens, B. G., & Verhaak, P. F. M. (2007). Cost-effectiveness of an activating intervention by social workers for patients with minor mental disorders on sick leave: A randomized controlled trial. *European Journal of Public Health, 17*(2), 214–220. doi:10.1093/eurpub/ckl099

Brown, C. H., Ten Have, T. R., Jo, B., Dagne, G., Wyman, P. A., Muthén, B., & Gibbons, R. D. (2009). Adaptive designs for randomized trials in public health. *Annual Review of Public Health, 30*, 1–25. doi:10.1146/annurev.publhealth.031308.100223

Brown, C. H., Wang, W., Kellam, S. G., Muthén, B. O., Petras, H., Toyinbo, P., . . . & the Prevention Science and Methodology Group. (2008). Methods for testing theory and evaluating impact in randomized field trials: Intent-to-treat analyses for integrating the perspectives of person, place, and time. *Drug and Alcohol Dependence, 95*(Suppl. 1), S74–S104. doi:10.1016/j.drugalcdep.2007.11.013

Brown, E. C., Graham, J. W., Hawkins, J. D., Arthur, M. W., Baldwin, M. M., Oesterle, S., . . . & Abbott, R. D. (2009). Design and analysis of the Community Youth Development Study longitudinal cohort sample. *Evaluation Review, 33*(4), 311–334. doi:10.1177/0193841X09337356

Brunette, M. F., Asher, D., Whitley, R., Lutz, W. J., Wieder, B. L., Jones, A. M., & McHugo, G. J. (2008). Implementation of integrated dual disorders treatment: A qualitative analysis of facilitators and barriers. *Psychiatric Services, 59*(9), 989–995. doi:10.1176/appi.ps.59.9.989

Brydon-Miller, M., & Greenwood, D. (2006). A re-examination of the relationship between action research and human subjects review processes. *Action Research, 4*(1), 117–128. doi:10.1177/1476750306060582

California Evidence-Based Clearinghouse for Child Welfare. (2011a). Michigan Family Reunification Program. http://www.cebc4cw.org/program/michigan-family-reunification-program/

California Evidence-Based Clearinghouse for Child Welfare. (2011b). Alcoholic Anonymous (A.A.). http://www.cebc4cw.org/program/alcoholics-anonymous/

Carden, F. (2009). *Knowledge to policy: Making the most of development research*. New Delhi, India: Sage.

Catalano, R. F., & Hawkins, J. D. (1996). The social development model: A theory of antisocial behavior. In J. D. Hawkins (Ed.), *Delinquency and crime: Current theories* (pp. 149–197). New York, NY: Cambridge University Press.

Chamberlain, P., Brown, C. H., Saldana, L., Reid, J., Wang, W., Marsenich, L., . . . & Bouwman, G. (2008). Engaging and recruiting counties in an experiment on implementing evidence-based practice in California. *Administration and Policy in Mental Health and Mental Health Services Research, 35*(4), 250–260. doi:10.1007/s10488-008-0167-x

Chamberlain, P., Leve, L. D., & DeGarmo, D. S. (2007). Multidimensional Treatment Foster Care for girls in the juvenile justice system: 2-year follow-up of a randomized clinical trial. *Journal of Consulting and Clinical Psychology, 75*(1), 187–193. doi:10.1037/0022-006X.75.1.187

Chamberlain, P., Price, J., Reid, J., & Landsverk, J. (2008). Cascading implementation of a foster and kinship parent intervention. *Child Welfare, 87*(5), 27–48.

Chan, D. (1998). Functional relations among constructs in the same content domain at different levels of analysis: A typology of composition models. *Journal of Applied Psychology, 83*(2), 234–246. doi:10.1037/0021-9010.83.2.234

Chorpita, B. F., Bernstein, A., Daleiden E. L., & the Research Network on Youth Mental Health. (2008). Driving with roadmaps and dashboards: Using information resources to structure the decision models in service organizations. *Administration and Policy in Mental Health and Mental Health Services Research, 35*(1–2), 114–123. doi:10.1007/s10488-007-0151-x

Chorpita, B. F., Daleiden, E. L., & Weisz, J. R. (2005). Modularity in the design and application of therapeutic interventions. *Applied and Preventive Psychology, 11*(3), 141–156. doi:10.1016/j.appsy.2005.05.002

Chorpita, B. F., Reise, S., Weisz, J. R., Grubbs, K., Becker, K. D., & Krull, J. L. (2010). Evaluation of the Brief Problem Checklist: Child and caregiver interviews to measure clinical progress. *Journal of Consulting and Clinical Psychology, 78*(4), 526–536. doi:10.1037/a0019602

Cochrane Effective Practice and Organisation of Care Review Group. (2002). *Data collection checklist.* http://epoc.cochrane.org/sites/epoc.cochrane.org/files/uploads/datacollectionchecklist.pdf

Collins, L. M., Murphy, S. A., Nair, V. N., & Strecher, V. J. (2005). A strategy for optimizing and evaluating behavioral interventions. *Annals of Behavioral Medicine, 30*(1), 65–73. doi:10.1207/s15324796abm3001_8

Concato, J., Shah, N., & Horwitz, R. I. (2000). Randomized, controlled trials, observational studies, and the hierarchy of research designs. *New England Journal of Medicine, 342*(25), 1887–1892.

Cooke, R. A., & Rousseau, D. M. (1988). Behavioral norms and expectations: A quantitative approach to the assessment of organizational culture. *Group & Organization Management, 13*(3): 245–273. doi:10.1177/105960118801300302

Crabtree, B. F., & Miller, W. L. (Eds.). (1992). *Doing qualitative research* (Vol. 3). Thousand Oaks, CA: Sage.

Cresswell, J. W. (1999). Mixed method research: Introduction and application. In G. J. Cizek (Ed.), *Handbook of educational policy* (pp. 455–472). San Diego, CA: Academic Press.

Cresswell, J. W., Fetters, M. D., & Ivankova, N. V. (2004). Designing a mixed methods study in primary care. *Annals of Family Medicine, 2*(1), 7–12. doi:10.1370/afm.104

Cresswell, J. W., & Plano Clark, V. L. (2007). *Designing and conducting mixed method research*. Thousand Oaks, CA: Sage.

Cresswell, J. W., Plano Clark, V. L., Gutmann, M. L., & Hanson, W. E. (2003). Advanced mixed methods research designs. In A. Tashakkori & C. Teddlie (Eds.), *Handbook of mixed methods in social and behavioral research* (pp. 209–240). Thousand Oaks, CA: Sage.

Currie, M., King, G., Rosenbaum, P., Law, M., Kertoy, M., & Specht, J. (2005). A model of impacts of research partnerships in health and social services. *Evaluation and Program Planning, 28*(4), 400–412. doi:10.1016/j.evalprogplan.2005.07.004

Damanpour, F. (1991). Organizational innovation: A meta-analysis of effects of determinants and moderators. *Academy of Management Journal, 34*(3), 555–590. doi:10.2307/256406

Dalton, H. L. (1989). AIDS in blackface. *Daedalus, 118*(3), 205–227.

Davies, H. T. O., Nutley, S. M., & Mannion, R. (2000). Organisational culture and quality of health care. *Quality in Health Care, 9*, 111–119. doi:10.1136/qhc.9.2.111

Dearing, J. W. (2008). Evolution of diffusion and dissemination theory. *Journal of Public Health Management and Practice, 14*(2), 99–108.

Demakis, J. G., McQueen, L., Kizer, K. W., & Feussner, J. R. (2000). Quality Enhancement Research Initiative (QUERI): A collaboration between research and clinical practice. *Medical Care, 38*(6, Suppl. I), I17–I25.

Denzin, N. K. (1978). *The research act: A theoretical introduction to sociological methods* (2nd ed.). New York, NY: McGraw-Hill.

Derogatis, L. R., Lipman, R. S., Rickels, K., Uhlenhuth, E. H., & Covi, L. (1974). The Hopkins Symptom Checklist (HSCL): A measure of primary symptom dimensions. *Modern Problems of Pharmacopsychiatry, 7*, 79–110.

Ell, K., Katon, W., Xie, B., Lee, P.-J., Kapetanovic, S., Guterman, J., & Chou, C.-P. (2010). Collaborative care management of major depression among low-income, predominately Hispanic subjects with diabetes: A randomized controlled trial. *Diabetes Care, 33*(4), 706–713. doi:10.2337/dc09–1711

Ell, K., Vourlekis, B., Xie, B., Nedjat-Haiem, F. R., Lee, P.-J., Muderspach, L., . . . & Palinkas, L. A. (2009). Cancer treatment adherence among low-income women with breast or gynecologic cancer. *Cancer, 115*(19), 4606–4615. doi:10.1002/cncr.24500

Fagan, A. A., Hanson, K., Hawkins, J. D., & Arthur, M. W. (2008). Bridging science to practice: Achieving prevention program implementation fidelity in the Community Youth Development Study. *American Journal of Community Psychology, 41*(3–4), 235–249. doi:10.1007/s10464–008–9176-x

Fagan, A. A., Hawkins, J. D., & Catalano, R. F. (2008). Using community epidemiological data to improve social settings: The Communities That Care prevention system. In M. Shinn & H. Yoshikawa (Eds.), *Toward positive youth development: Transforming schools and community programs.* New York, NY: Oxford University Press.

Federal Coordinating Council for Comparative Effectiveness Research. (2009). *Report to the president and the Congress.* Washington, DC: Department of Health and Human Services. http://www.hhs.gov/recovery/programs/cer/cerannualrpt.pdf

Ferlie, E. B., & Shortell, S. M. (2001). Improving the quality of health care in the United Kingdom and the United States: A framework for change. *Milbank Quarterly, 79*(2), 281–315. doi:10.1111/1468–0009.00206

Flay, B. R. (1986). Efficacy and effectiveness trials (and other phases of research) in the development of health promotion programs. *Preventive Medicine, 15*(5), 451–474. doi:10.1016/0091–7435(86)90024–1

Fixsen, D. L., Blase, K. A., Naoom, S. F., & Wallace, F. (2009). Core implementation components. *Research on Social Work Practice, 19*(5), 531–540. doi:10.1177/1049731509335549

Fixsen, D. L., Naoom, S. F., Blase, K. A., Friedman, R. M., & Wallace, F. (2005). *Implementation research: A synthesis of the literature* (FMHI Publication No. 231). Tampa, FL: National Implementation Research Network, Louis de la Parte Florida Mental Health Institute, University of South Florida.

Frambach, R. T., & Schillewaert, N. (2002). Organizational innovation adoption: A multi-level framework of determinants and opportunities for future research. *Journal of Business Research,* *55*(2), 163–176. doi:10.1016/S0148-2963(00)00152-1

French, W. L., & Bell, C. H., Jr. (1998). *Organization development: Behavior science interventions for organization improvement* (6th ed.). Upper Saddle River, NJ: Prentice Hall.

Frueh, B. C., Cusack, K. J., Grubaugh, A. L., Sauvageot, J. A., & Wells, C. (2006). Clinicians' perspectives on cognitive-behavioral treatment for PTSD among persons with severe mental illness. *Psychiatric Services, 57*(7), 1027–1031. doi:10.1176/appi.ps.57.7.1027

Garber, A. M., & Meltzer, D. O. (2009). Setting priorities for comparative effectiveness research. In *Implementing comparative effectiveness research: Priorities, methods, and impact* (pp. 15–34). Washington, DC: Engelberg Center for Health Care Reform, Brookings Institution.

Gibbs, L. E. (2003). *Evidence-based practice for the helping professions: A practical guide with integrated multimedia.* Pacific Grove, CA: Thomson Brooks/Cole.

Gibbons, M., Limoges, C., Nowotny, H., Schwartzman, S., Scott, P., & Trow, M. (1994). *The new production of knowledge: The dynamics of science and research in contemporary societies.* London, England: Sage.

Gioia, D., & Dziadosz, G. (2008). Adoption of evidence-based practices in community mental health: A mixed-method study of practitioner experience. *Community Mental Health Journal, 44*(5), 347–357. doi:10.1007/s10597-008-9136-9

Glaser, B. G., & Strauss, A. L. (1967). *The discovery of grounded theory: Strategies for qualitative research.* Hawthorne, NY: Aldine de Gruyter.

Glasgow, R. E. (2009). Critical measurement issues in translational research. *Research on Social Work Practice, 19*(5), 560–568. doi:10.1177/1049731509335497

Glasgow, R. E., Magid, D. J., Beck, A., Ritzwoller, D., & Estabrooks, P. A. (2005). Practical clinical trials for translating research to practice: Design and measurement recommendations. *Medical Care, 43*(6), 551–557.

Glazerman, S., Levy, D. M., & Myers, D. (2003). Nonexperimental versus experimental estimates of earnings impacts. *Annals of the American Academy of Political and Social Science, 589*(1), 63–93. doi:10.1177/0002716203254879

Glisson, C. (1989). The effect of leadership on workers in human service organizations. *Administration in Social Work, 13*(3–4), 99–116. doi:10.1300/J147v13n03_06

Glisson, C. (1992). Structure and technology in human service organizations. In Y. Hasenfeld (Ed.), *Human services as complex organizations* (pp. 184–202). Newbury Park, CA: Sage.

Glisson, C. (2002). The organizational context of children's mental health services. *Clinical Child and Family Psychology Review, 5*(4), 233–253.

Glisson, C., Dukes, D., & Green, P. (2006). The effects of the ARC organizational intervention on caseworker turnover, climate, and culture in children's service systems. *Child Abuse & Neglect, 30*(8), 855–880. doi:10.1016/j.chiabu.2005.12.010

Glisson, C., & Durick, M. (1988). Predictors of job satisfaction and organizational commitment in human service organizations. *Administrative Science Quarterly, 33*(1), 61–81.

Glisson, C., & Green, P. (2006). The effects of organizational culture and climate on the access to mental health care in child welfare and juvenile justice systems. *Administration and Policy in Mental Health and Mental Health Services Research, 33*(4), 433–448. doi:10.1007/s10488-005-0016-0

Glisson, C., & Hemmelgarn, A. (1998). The effects of organizational climate and interorganizational coordination on the quality and outcomes of children's service systems. *Child Abuse & Neglect, 22*(5), 401–421. doi:10.1016/S0145-2134(98)00005-2

Glisson, C., & James, L. R. (2002). The cross-level effects of culture and climate in human service teams. *Journal of Organizational Behavior, 23*(6), 767–794. doi:10.1002/job.162

Glisson, C., Landsverk, J., Schoenwald, S. K., Kelleher, K. Hoagwood, K. E., Mayberg, S., . . . & the Research Network on Youth Mental Health. (2008). Assessing the organizational social context (OSC) of mental health services: Implications for research and practice. *Administration and Policy in Mental Health and Mental Health Services Research, 35*(1–2), 98–113. doi:10.1007/s10488-007-0148-5

Glisson, C., & Schoenwald, S. K. (2005). The ARC organizational and community intervention strategy for implementing evidence-based children's mental health treatments. *Mental Health Services Research, 7*(4), 243–259. doi:10.1007/s11020-005-7456-1

Glisson, C., Schoenwald, S. K., Hemmelgarn, A., Green, P., Dukes, D., Armstrong, K. S., & Chapman, J. E. (2010). Randomized trial of MST and ARC in a two-level evidence-based treatment implementation strategy. *Journal of Consulting and Clinical Psychology, 78*(4), 537–550. doi:10.1037/a0019160

Glisson, C., Schoenwald, S. K., Kelleher, K., Landsverk, J., Hoagwood, K. E., Mayberg, S., . . . & the Research Network on Youth Mental Health. (2008). Therapist turnover and new program sustainability in mental health clinics as a function of organizational culture, climate, and service structure. *Administration and Policy in Mental Health and Mental Health Services Research, 35*(1–2), 124–133. doi:10.1007/s10488–007–0152–9

Green, L. W., & Kreuter, M. W. (2005). *Health program planning: An educational and ecological approach.* Boston, MA: McGraw-Hill.

Green, L. W., Ottoson, J. M., Garcia, C., & Hiatt, R. A. (2009). Diffusion theory and knowledge dissemination, utilization, and integration in public health. *Annual Review of Public Health, 30,* 151–174. doi:10.1146/annurev.publhealth.031308.100049

Greenberg, M. T., Feinberg, M. E., Gomez, B. J., & Osgood, D. W. (2005). Testing a community prevention focused model of coalition functioning and sustainability: A comprehensive study of Communities That Care in Pennsylvania. In T. Stockwell, P. Gruenewald, J. Toumbourou, & W. Loxley (Eds.), *Preventing harmful substance use: The evidence base for policy and practice* (pp. 129–142). Chichester, England: John Wiley & Sons.

Greene, J. C., Caracelli, V. J., & Graham, W. F. (1989). Toward a conceptual framework for mixed-method evaluation designs. *Educational Evaluation and Policy Analysis, 11*(3), 255–274. doi:10.3102/01623737011003255

Greenhalgh, T. (2001). *How to read a paper: The basics of evidence-based medicine.* London, England: BMJ Books.

Greenhalgh, T., Robert, G., Macfarlane, F., Bate, P., & Kyriakidou, O. (2004). Diffusion of innovations in service organizations: Systematic review and recommendations. *Milbank Quarterly, 82*(4), 581–629. doi:10.1111/j.0887-378X.2004.00325.x

Griswold, K. S., Zayas, L. E., Pastore, P. A., Smith, S. J., Wagner, C. M., & Servoss, T. J. (2008). Primary care after psychiatric crisis: A qualitative analysis. *Annals of Family Medicine, 6*(1), 38–43. doi:10.1370/afm.760

Grol, R. P., Bosch, M. C., Hulscher, M. E., Eccles, M. P., & Wensing, M. (2007). Planning and studying improvement in patient care: The use of theoretical perspectives. *Milbank Quarterly, 85*(1), 93–138. doi:10.1111/j.1468-0009.2007.00478.x

Grol, R. P., & Grimshaw, J. (1999). Evidence-based implementation of evidence-based medicine. *The Joint Commission Journal on Quality Improvement, 25*(10), 503–513.

Grol, R. P., & Grimshaw, J. (2003). From best evidence to best practice: Effective implementation of change in patients' care. *Lancet, 362*(9391), 1225–1230. doi:10.1016/S0140-6736(03)14546-1

Guo, S., & Fraser, W. M. (2009). *Propensity score analysis: Statistical methods and applications.* Thousand Oaks, CA: Sage.

Hall, G. C. N. (2001). Psychotherapy research with ethnic minorities: Empirical, ethical, and conceptual issues. *Journal of Consulting and Clinical Psychology, 69*(3), 502–510. doi:10.1037/0022-006X.69.3.502

Harris, K. J., Jerome, N. W., & Fawcett, S. B. (1997). Rapid assessment procedures: A review and critique. *Human Organization, 56*(3), 375–378.

Hatch, J., Moss, N., Saran, A., Presley-Cantrell, L., & Mallory, C. (1993). Community research: Partnership in black communities. *American Journal of Preventive Medicine, 9*(6, Suppl.), 27–31.

Hawkins, J. D., Brown, E. C., Oesterle, S., Arthur, M. W., Abbott, R. D., & Catalano, R. F. (2008). Early effects of Communities That Care on targeted risks and initiation of delinquent behavior and substance use. *Journal of Adolescent Health, 43*(1), 15–22. doi:10.1016/j.jadohealth.2008.01.022

Hawkins, J. D., & Catalano, R. F. (2002). *Investing in your community's youth: An introduction to the Communities That Care system.* South Deerfield, MA: Channing Bete.

Hawkins, J. D., Catalano, R. F., & Arthur, M. W. (2002). Promoting science-based prevention in communities. *Addictive Behaviors, 27*(6), 951–976. doi:10.1016/S0306-4603(02)00298-8

Hawkins, J. D., Catalano, R. F., Arthur, M. W., Egan, E., Brown, E. C., Abbott, R. D., & Murray, D. M. (2008). Testing Communities That Care: The rationale, design, and behavioral baseline equivalence of the Community Youth Development Study. *Prevention Science, 9*(3), 178–190. doi:10.1007/s11121-008-0092-y

Hawkins, J. D., Catalano, R. F., & Associates. (1992). *Communities That Care: Action for drug abuse prevention* (1st ed.). San Francisco, CA: Jossey-Bass.

Hawkins, J. D., Guo, J., Hill, K. G., Battin-Pearson, S., & Abbott, R. D. (2001). Long-term effects of the Seattle Social Development intervention on school bonding trajectories. *Applied Developmental Science, 5*(4), 225–236. doi:10.1207/S1532480XADS0504_04

Hawkins, J. D., Oesterle, S., Brown, E. C., Arthur, M. W., Abbott, R. D., Fagan, A. A., & Catalano, R. F. (2009). Results of a type 2 translational research trial to prevent adolescent drug use and delinquency: A test of Communities That Care. *Archives of Pediatrics and Adolescent Medicine, 163*(9), 789–798.

Hawkins, J. D., & Weis, J. G. (1985). The social development model: An integrated approach to delinquency prevention. *Journal of Primary Prevention, 6*(2), 73–97. doi:10.1007/BF01325432

Healy, K. (2001). Participatory action research and social work: A critical appraisal. *International Social Work, 44*(1), 93–105. doi:10.1177/002087280104400108

Hedeker, D., & Gibbons, R. D. (2006). *Longitudinal data analysis.* Hoboken, NJ: John Wiley & Sons.

Hemmelgarn, A. L., Glisson, C., & Dukes, D. (2001). Emergency room culture and the emotional support component of family-centered care. *Children's Health Care, 30*(2), 93–110. doi:10.1207/S15326888CHC3002_2

Henke, R. M., Chou, A. F., Chanin, J. C., Zides, A. B., & Scholle, S. H. (2008). Physician attitude toward depression care interventions: Implications for implementation of quality improvement initiatives. *Implementation Science, 3.* doi:10.1186/1748-5908-3-40

Higgins, J. P. T., & Green, S. (Eds.). (2008). *Cochrane handbook for systematic review of interventions.* Hoboken, NJ: John Wiley & Sons.

Hoagwood, K. E., Vogel, J. M., Levitt, J. M., D'Amico, P. J., Paisner, W. I., & Kaplan, S. J. (2007). Implementing an evidence-based trauma treatment in a state system after September 11: The CATS Project. *Journal of the American Academy of Child and Adolescent Psychiatry, 46*(6), 773–779. doi:10.1097/chi.0b013e3180413def

Horowitz, C. R., Robinson, M., & Seifer, S. (2009). Community-based participatory research from the margin to the mainstream: Are researchers prepared? *Circulation: Journal of the American Heart Association, 119*, 2633–2642. doi:10.1161/CIRCULATIONAHA.107.729863

Horwitz, S. M., Chamberlain, P., Landsverk, J., & Mullican, C. (2010). Improving the mental health of children in child welfare through the implementation of evidence-based parenting interventions. *Administration and Policy in Mental Health and Mental Health Services Research, 37*(1–2), 27–39. doi:10.1007/s10488-010-0274-3

Hovmand, P. S., & Gillespie, D. F. (2008). Implementation of evidence-based practice and organizational performance. *Journal of Behavioral Health Services and Research, 37*(1), 79–94. doi:10.1007/s11414-008-9154-y

Institute for Healthcare Improvement. (2004). The Breakthrough Series: IHI's collaborative model for achieving breakthrough improvement. *Diabetes Spectrum, 17*(2), 97–101. doi:10.2337/diaspect.17.2.97

Institute of Medicine. (2001). *Crossing the quality chasm: A new health system for the 21st century.* Washington, DC: National Academies Press.

International Federation of Social Workers. (2000). *Definition of social work.* Retrieved from http://www.ifsw.org/en/p38000208.html

Israel, B. A., Eng, E., Schulz, A. J., & Parker, E. A. (Eds.). (2005). *Methods in community-based participatory research for health.* San Francisco, CA: Jossey-Bass.

Israel, B. A., Schulz, A. J., Parker, E. A., & Becker, A. B. (1998). Review of community-based research: Assessing partnership approaches to improve public health. *Annual Review of Public Health, 19,* 173–202. doi:10.1146/annurev.publhealth.19.1.173

Israel, B. A., Schulz, A. J., Parker, E. A., Becker, A. B., Allen, A. J., III, & Guzman, J. R. (2003). Critical issues in developing and following community based participatory research principles. In M. Minkler & N. Wallerstein (Eds.), *Community-based participatory research for health* (pp. 53–76). San Francisco, CA: Jossey-Bass.

James, L. A., & James, L. R. (1989). Integrating work environment perceptions: Explorations into the measurement of meaning. *Journal of Applied Psychology, 74*(5), 739–751. doi:10.1037/0021-9010.74.5.739

James, L. R. (1982). Aggregation bias in estimates of perceptual agreement. *Journal of Applied Psychology, 67*(2), 219–229. doi:10.1037/0021-9010.67.2.219

Jensen, J. M., Dieterich, W. A., Brisson, D., Bender, K. A., & Powell, A. (2010). Preventing childhood bullying: Findings and lessons from the Denver Public Schools Trial. *Research on Social Work Practice, 20*(5), 509–517. doi:10.1177/1049731509359186

Jones, A. P., & James, L. R. (1979). Psychological climate: Dimensions and relationships of individual and aggregated work environment perceptions. *Organizational Behavior and Human Performance, 23*(2), 201–250. doi:10.1016/0030-5073(79)90056-4

Jones, B. L., Pomeroy, E. C., & Sampson, M. (2009). University-community partnerships and community-based participatory research: One community's approach to enhance capacity in end-of-life and bereavement practice, research, and education. *Journal* of *Social Work in End-of-Life & Palliative Care*, 5(1–2), 94–104. doi:10.1080/15524250903173926

Jones, L., & Wells, K. B. (2007). Strategies for academic and clinician engagement in community-participatory partnered research. *Journal of the American Medical Association*, 297(4), 407–410. doi:10.1001/jama.297.4.407

Jonkman, H. B., Haggerty, K. P., Steketee, M., Fagan, A., Hanson, K., & Hawkins, J. D. (2008). Communities That Care, core elements and context: Research of implementation in two countries. *Social Development Issues*, 30(3), 42–57.

Joyce, W. F., & Slocum, J. W. (1984). Collective climate: Agreement as a basis for defining aggregate climates in organizations. *Academy of Management Journal*, 27(4), 721–742.

Judge, T. A., Thoresen, C. J., Pucik, V., & Welbourne, T. M. (1999). Managerial coping with organizational change: A dispositional perspective. *Journal of Applied Psychology*, 84(1), 107–122. doi:10.1037/0021-9010.84.1.107

Kelly, J. A., Somlai, A. M., DiFranceisco, W. J., Otto-Salaj, L. L., McAuliffe, T. L., Hackl, K. L., Heckman, T. G., . . . & Rompa, D. (2000). Bridging the gap between the science and service of HIV prevention: Transferring effective research-based HIV prevention interventions to community AIDS service providers. *American Journal of Public Health*, 90(7), 1082–1088. doi:10.2105/AJPH.90.7.1082

Kendall, P. C. (1990). *The Coping Cat workbook*. Ardmore, PA: Workbook Publishing.

Killaspy, H., Johnson, S., Pierce, B., Bebbington, P., Pilling, S., Nolan, F., & King, M. (2009). Successful engagement: A mixed methods study of the approaches of assertive community treatment and community mental health teams in the REACT trial. *Social Psychiatry and Psychiatric Epidemiology*, 44(7), 532–540. doi:10.1007/s00127-008-0472-4

Kimberly, J., & Cook, J. M. (2008). Organizational measurement and the implementation of innovations in mental health services. *Administration and Policy in Mental Health and Mental Health Services Research*, 35(1–2), 11–20. doi:10.1007/s10488-007-0143-x

King, G., Servais, M., Kertoy, M., Specht, J., Currie, M., Rosenbaum, P., . . . & Willoughby, T. (2009). A measure of community members' perceptions of the impacts of research partnerships in health and social services. *Evaluation and Program Planning*, 32(3), 289–299. doi:10.1016/j.evalprogplan.2009.02.002

Klein, K. J., & Knight, A. P. (2005). Innovation implementation: Overcoming the challenge. *Current Directions in Psychological Science, 14*(5), 243–246.

Klein, K. J., & Sorra, J. S. (1996). The challenge of innovation implementation. *Academy of Management Review, 21*(4), 1055–1080.

Knipschild, P. (1994). Systematic reviews: Some examples. *British Medical Journal, 309*, 719–721.

Kramer, M. S. (1988). *Clinical epidemiology and biostatistics.* Berlin, NY: Springer-Verlag.

Landsverk, J., Brown, C. H., Reutz, J. R., Palinkas, L. A., & Horwitz, S. M. (2011). Design elements in implementation research: A structured review of child welfare and child mental health studies. *Administration and Policy in Mental Health and Mental Health Services Research, 38*(1), 54–63. doi:10.1007/s10488-010-0315-y

Lave, J., & Wenger, E. (1991). *Situated learning: Legitimate peripheral participation.* Cambridge, England: Cambridge University Press.

Lehman, W. E. K., Greener, J. M., & Simpson, D. D. (2002). Assessing organizational readiness for change. *Journal of Substance Abuse Treatment, 22*(4), 197–209. doi:10.1016/S0740-5472(02)00233-7

Leschied, A., & Cunningham, A. (2002). *Seeking effective interventions for serious young offenders: Interim results of a four-year randomized study of Multisystemic Therapy in Ontario, Canada.* London, Canada: Centre for Children & Families in the Justice System.

Letcher, A. S., & Perlow, K. M. (2009). Community-based participatory research shows how a community initiative creates networks to improve well-being. *American Journal of Preventive Medicine, 37*(6, Suppl. 1), S292–S299. doi:10.1016/j.amepre.2009.08.008

Liang, K.-Y., & Zeger, S. L. (1986). Longitudinal data analysis using generalized linear models. *Biometrika, 73*(1), 13–22. doi:10.1093/biomet/73.1.13

Lindamer, L. A., Lebowitz, B. D., Hough, R. L., Garcia, P., Aquirre, A., Halpain, M. C., . . . & Jeste, D. V. (2008). Public-academic partnerships: Improving care for older persons with schizophrenia through an academic-community partnership. *Psychiatric Services, 59*(3), 236–239. doi:10.1176/appi.ps.59.3.236

Lipsey, M. W., & Wilson, D. B. (1993). The efficacy of psychological, educational, and behavioral treatment: Confirmation from meta-analysis. *American Psychologist, 48*(12), 1181–1209.

Littell, J. H., Campbell, M., Green, S., & Toews, B. (2005). *Multisystemic Therapy for social, emotional, and behavioral problems in youth aged 10–17. Cochrane Database of Systematic Reviews, 2005*(4). doi:10.1002/14651858.CD004797.pub4

Lomas, J. (1993). Diffusion, dissemination, and implementation: Who should do what? *Annals of the New York Academy of Sciences, 703*, 226–237. doi:10.1111/j.1749-6632.1993.tb26351.x

Lutzker, J. R., & Bigelow, K. M. (2002). *Reducing child maltreatment: A guidebook for parent services.* New York, NY: Guilford Press.

Lutzker, J. R., & Rice, J. M. (1984). Project 12-Ways: Measuring outcome of a large in-home service for treatment and prevention of child abuse and neglect. *Child Abuse & Neglect, 8*(4), 519–524. doi:10.1016/0145-2134(84)90034-6

Macaulay, A. C., Commanda, L. E., Freeman, W. L., Gibson, N., McCabe, M. L., Robbins, C. M., & Twohig, P. L. (1999). Participatory research maximises community and lay involvement. *British Medical Journal, 319*(7212), 774–778.

Madison, S. M., McKay, M. M., Paikoff, R., & Bell, C. C. (2000). Basic research and community collaboration: Necessary ingredients for the development of a family-based HIV prevention program. *AIDS Education and Prevention, 12*(4), 281–298.

Manuel, J. I., Mullen, E. J., Fang, L., Bellamy, J. L., & Bledsoe, S. E. (2009). Preparing social work practitioners to use evidence-based practice: A comparison of experiences from an implementation project. *Research on Social Work Practice, 19*(5), 613–627. doi:10.1177/1049731509335547

Marshall, T., Rapp, C. A., Becker, D. R., & Bond, G. R. (2008). Key factors for implementing supported employment. *Psychiatric Services, 59*(8), 886–892. doi:10.1176/appi.ps.59.8.886

Marty, D., Rapp, C., McHugo, G., & Whitley, R. (2008). Factors influencing consumer outcome monitoring in implementation of evidence-based practices: Results from the National EBP Implementation Project. *Administration and Policy in Mental Health and Mental Health Services Research, 35*(3), 204–211. doi:10.1007/s10488-007-0157-4

McArdle, J. J., & Hamagami, F. (1996). Multilevel models from a multiple group structural equation perspective. In G. A. Marcoulides & R. E. Schumacker (Eds.), *Advanced structural equation modeling: Issues and techniques* (pp. 89–124). Mahwah, NJ: Lawrence Erlbaum Associates.

McCulloch, C. E., & Searle, S. R. (2001). *Generalized, linear, and mixed models.* New York, NY: John Wiley & Sons.

McGlynn, E. A., Asch, S. M., Adams, J., Keesey, J., Hicks, J., DeCristofaro, A., & Kerr, E. A. (2003). The quality of health care delivered to adults in the United States. *New England Journal of Medicine, 348*(26), 2635–2645.

McHugo, G. J., Drake, R. E., Whitley, R., Bond, G. R., Campbell, K., Rapp, C. A., . . . & Finnerty, M. T. (2007). Fidelity outcomes in the National Implementing Evidence-Based Practices Project. *Psychiatric Services, 58*(10), 1279–1284. doi:10.1176/appi.ps.58.10.1279

McKay, M. M., Gopalan, G., Franco, L. M., Kalogerogiannis, K., Umpierre, M., Olshtain-Mann, O., . . . & Goldstein, L. (2010). It takes a village to deliver and test child and family-focused services. *Research on Social Work Practice, 20*(5), 476–482. doi:10.1177/1049731509360976

Mendel, P., Meredith, L. S., Schoenbaum, M., Sherbourne, C. D., & Wells, K. B. (2008). Interventions in organizational and community context: A framework for building evidence on dissemination and implementation in health services research. *Administration and Policy in Mental Health and Mental Health Services Research, 35*(1–2), 21–37. doi:10.1007/s10488-007-0144-9

Michie, S., Fixsen, D., Grimshaw, J. M., & Eccles, M. P. (2009). Specifying and reporting complex behaviour change interventions: The need for a scientific method. *Implementation Science, 4.* doi:10.1186/1748-5908-4-40

Miles, M. B., & Huberman, A. M. (1994). *Qualitative data analysis: An expanded sourcebook* (2nd ed.). Thousand Oaks, CA: Sage.

Miller, R. L., & Shinn, M. (2005). Learning from communities: Overcoming difficulties in dissemination of prevention and promotion efforts. *American Journal of Community Psychology, 35*(3–4), 169–183. doi:10.1007/s10464-005-3395-1

Miller, W. L., & Crabtree, B. F. (2005). Healing landscapes: Patients, relationships, and creating optimal healing places. *Journal of Alternative and Complementary Medicine, 11*(Suppl. 1), S41–S49.

Minkler, M., & Wallerstein, N. (Eds.). (2003). *Community-based participatory research for health.* San Francisco, CA: Jossey-Bass.

Mitton, C., Simpson, L., Gardner, L., Barnes, F., & McDougall, G. (2007). Calgary Diversion Program: A community-based alternative to incarceration for mentally ill offenders. *Journal of Mental Health Policy and Economics, 10*(3), 145–151.

Moffatt, S., White, M., Mackintosh, J., & Howell, D. (2006). Using quantitative and qualitative data in health services research–what happens when mixed method findings conflict? *BMC Health Services Research, 6*(28). doi:10.1186/1472–6963–6–28

Morgan, D. L. (1998). Practical strategies for combining qualitative and quantitative methods: Applications to health research. *Qualitative Health Research, 8*(3), 362–376. doi:10.1177/104973239800800307

Morse, J. M. (1991). Approaches to qualitative-quantitative methodological triangulation. *Nursing Research, 40*(2), 120–123.

Morse, J. M. (2003). Principles of mixed methods and multimethod research design. In A. Tashakkori & C. Teddlie (Eds.), *Handbook of mixed methods in social and behavioral research* (pp. 189–208). Thousand Oaks, CA: Sage.

Mowday, R. T., Porter, L. W., & Steers, R. M. (1982). *Employee-organization linkages: The psychology of commitment, absenteeism, and turnover.* New York, NY: Academic Press.

Mrazek, P. J., & Haggerty, R. J. (Eds.). (1994). *Reducing risks for mental disorders: Frontiers for preventive intervention research.* Washington, DC: National Academies Press.

Murphy, S. A., Lynch, K. G., Oslin, D., McKay, J. R., & Ten Have, T. R. (2007). Developing adaptive treatment strategies in substance abuse research. *Drug and Alcohol Dependence, 88*(Suppl. 2), S24–S30. doi:10.1016/j.drugalcdep.2006.09.008

Muthusamy, S. K., & White, M. A. (2005). Learning and knowledge transfer in strategic alliances: A social exchange view. *Organization Studies, 26*(3), 415–441. doi:10.1177/0170840605050874

Nastasi, B. K., & Hitchcock, J. (2009). Challenges of evaluating multilevel interventions. *American Journal of Community Psychology, 43*(3–4), 360–376. doi:10.1007/s10464–009–9239–7

National Advisory Mental Health Council. (1998). *Bridging science and service: A report by the National Advisory Mental Health Council's Clinical Treatment and Services Research Workgroup* (NIH Publication No. 99–4353). Bethesda, MD: National Institutes of Health/ National Institute of Mental Health.

National Advisory Mental Health Council. (2000). *Translating behavioral science into action: Report of the National Advisory Mental Health Council's Behavioral Science Workgroup* (NIH Publication No. 00–4699). Bethesda, MD: National Institutes of Health/National Institute of Mental Health.

National Advisory Mental Health Council. (2001). *Blueprint for change: Research on child and adolescent mental health. Report of the National*

Advisory Mental Health Council's Workgroup on Child and Adolescent Mental Health Intervention Development and Deployment. Bethesda, MD: National Institutes of Health/National Institute of Mental Health.

National Association of Social Workers. (2008). *Code of ethics.* Retrieved from http://www.socialworkers.org/pubs/code/default.asp

National Institutes of Health. (2009). *NIH Roadmap for Medical Research.* Bethesda, MD: National Institutes of Health. Retrieved from. http://commonfund.nih.gov/aboutroadmap.aspx

National Institute of Mental Health. (2004). *Advancing the science of implementation: Improving the fit between mental health intervention development and service systems.* Retrieved from http://wwwapps.nimh.nih.gov/research-funding/scientific-meetings/2004/advancing-the-science-of-implementation.shtml

Necheles, J. W., Chung, E. Q., Hawes-Dawson, J., Ryan, G. W., Williams, L. B., Holmes, H. N., . . . Schuster, M. A. (2007). The Teen Photovoice Project: A pilot study to promote health through advocacy. *Progress in Community Health Partnerships: Research, Education, and Action, 1*(3), 221–229. doi:10.1353/cpr.2007.0027

Nelson, T. D., & Steele, R. G. (2007). Predictors of practitioner self-reported use of evidence-based practices: Practitioner training, clinical setting, and attitudes toward research. *Administration and Policy in Mental Health and Mental Health Services Research, 34*(4), 319–330. doi:10.1007/s10488–006–0111-x

Nelson, T. D., Steele, R. G., & Mize, J. A. (2006). Practitioner attitudes toward evidence-based practice: Themes and challenges. *Administration and Policy in Mental Health and Mental Health Services Research, 33*(3), 398–409. doi:10.1007/s10488–006–0044–4

Newman, I., & Benz, C. R. (1998). *Qualitative-quantitative research methodology: Exploring the interactive continuum.* Carbondale, IL: Southern Illinois University Press.

Nutley, S. M., Walter, I., & Davies, H. T. O. (2007). *Using evidence: How research can inform public services.* Bristol, England: Policy Press.

O'Connell, M. E., Boat, T., & Warner, K. E. (Eds.). (2009). *Preventing mental, emotional, and behavioral disorders among young people: Progress and possibilities.* Washington, DC: National Academies Press.

Ogden, T., & Hagen, K. A. (2006). Virker MST? Kommentarer til en systematisk forskningsoversikt og meta-analyse av MST. *Nordisk Socialt Arbeid, 26*(3), 222–233.

Painter, K. (2009). Multisystemic Therapy as community-based treatment for youth with severe emotional disturbance. *Research on Social Work Practice, 19*(3), 314–324. doi:10.1177/1049731508318772

Palinkas, L. A. (2009, May). *Social networks and implementation of evidence-based practices in public youth-serving systems*. Presented at the meeting of the Society for Prevention Research, Washington, DC.

Palinkas, L. A. (2010). Commentary: Cultural adaptation, collaboration, and exchange. *Research on Social Work Practice, 20*(5), 544–546. doi:10.1177/1049731510366145

Palinkas, L. A., & Aarons, G. A. (2009). A view from the top: Executive and management challenges in a statewide implementation of an evidence-based practice to reduce child neglect. *International Journal of Child Health and Human Development, 2*(1), 47–55.

Palinkas, L. A., Aarons, G. A., Chorpita, B. F., Hoagwood, K., Landsverk, J., & Weisz, J. R. (2009). Cultural exchange and the implementation of evidence-based practices: Two case studies. *Research on Social Work Practice, 19*(5), 602–612. doi:10.1177/1049731509335529

Palinkas, L. A., Aarons, G. A., Horwitz, S. M., Chamberlain, P., Hurlburt, M., & Landsverk, J. (2011). Mixed method designs in implementation research. *Administration and Policy in Mental Health and Mental Health Services Research, 38*(1), 44–53. doi:10.1007/s10488–010–0314-z

Palinkas, L. A., Allred, C., & Landsverk, J. (2005). Models of research-operational collaboration for behavioral health in space. *Aviation, Space and Environmental Medicine, 76*(6, Suppl. 1), B52–B60.

Palinkas, L. A., Criado, V., Fuentes, D., Shepherd, S., Milian, H., Folsom, D., & Jeste, D. V. (2007). Unmet needs for services for older adults with mental illness: Comparison of views of different stakeholder groups. *American Journal of Geriatric Psychiatry, 15*(6), 530–540. doi:10.1097/JGP.0b013e3180381505

Palinkas, L. A., Fuentes, D., Holloway, I., Wu, Q., & Chamberlain, P. (2010, July). *Advice networks and implementation of evidence-based practices in public youth-serving systems*. Presented at Sunbelt XXX, International Network for Social Network Analysis Conference, Riva del Garda, Italy.

Palinkas, L. A., Horwitz, S. M., Chamberlain, P., Hurlburt, M., & Landsverk, J. (2011). Mixed-methods designs in mental health services research: A review. *Psychiatric Services, 63*(3), 255–263. doi:10.1176/appi.ps.62.3.255

Palinkas, L. A., Prussing, E., Landsverk, J., & Reznik, V. M. (2003). Youth violence prevention in the aftermath of the San Diego East County school shootings: A qualitative assessment of community explanatory models. *Ambulatory Pediatrics, 3*(5), 246–252. doi:10.1367/1539–4409(2003)003<0246:YPITAO>2.0.CO;2

Palinkas, L. A., Prussing, E., Reznik, V. M., & Landsverk, J. (2004). The San Diego East County school shootings: A qualitative study of community level post-traumatic stress. *Prehospital and Disaster Medicine, 19*(1), 113–121.

Palinkas, L. A., Schoenwald, S. K., Hoagwood, K., Landsverk, J., Chorpita, B. F., Weisz, J. R., & the Research Network on Youth Mental Health. (2008). An ethnographic study of implementation of evidence-based treatments in child mental health: First steps. *Psychiatric Services, 59*(7), 738–746. doi:10.1176/appi.ps.59.7.738

Patton, M. Q. (2001). *Qualitative research and evaluation methods* (3rd ed.). Thousand Oaks, CA: Sage.

Petrosino, A., Turpin-Petrosino, C., & Buehler, J. (2004). *"Scared Straight" and other juvenile awareness programs for preventing juvenile delinquency.* Retrieved from Campbell Collaboration Library of Systematic Reviews website: http://www.campbellcollaboration.org/lib/download/13/

Petrucci, C. J., & Quinlan, K. M. (2007). Bridging the research-practice gap: Concept mapping as a mixed-methods strategy in practice-based research and evaluation. *Journal of Social Service Research, 34*(2), 25–42. doi:10.1300/J079v34n02_03

Petticrew, M., & Roberts, H. (2006). *Systematic reviews in the social sciences: A practical guide.* Oxford, England: Blackwell.

Pinto, R. M., McKay, M. M., & Escobar, C. (2008). "You've gotta know the community": Minority women make recommendations about community-focused health research. *Women & Health, 47*(1), 83–104. doi:10.1300/J013v47n01_05

Poduska, J., Kellam, S., Brown, C. H., Ford, C., Windham, A., Keegan, N., & Wang, W. (2009). Study protocol for a group randomized controlled trial of a classroom-based intervention aimed at preventing early risk factors for drug abuse: Integrating effectiveness and implementation research. *Implementation Science, 4.* doi:10.1186/1748–5908-4–56

President's New Freedom Commission on Mental Health. (2003). *Achieving the promise: Transforming mental health care in America* (Final Report, DHHS Publication No. SMA-03–3823). Rockville, MD: Department of Health and Human Services.

Proctor, E. K., Hascke, L., Morrow-Howell, N., Shumway, M., & Snell, G. (2008). Perceptions about competing psychosocial problems and treatment priorities among older adults with depression. *Psychiatric Services, 59*(6), 670–675. doi:10.1176/appi.ps.59.6.670

Proctor, E. K., Knudsen, K. J., Fedoravicius, N., Hovmand, P., Rosen, A., & Perron, B. (2007). Implementation of evidence-based practice in community behavioral health: Agency director perspectives. *Administration and Policy in Mental Health and Mental Health Services Research, 34*(5), 479–488. doi:10.1007/s10488-007-0129-8

Proctor, E. K., Landsverk, J., Aarons, G., Chambers, D., Glisson, C., & Mittman, B. (2009). Implementation research in mental health services: An emerging science with conceptual, methodological, and training challenges. *Administration and Policy in Mental Health and Mental Health Services Research, 36*(1), 24–34. doi:10.1007/s10488-008-0197-4

Proctor, E. K., Silmere, H., Raghavan, R., Hovmand, P., Aarons, G., Bunger, A., . . . & Hensley, M. (2010). Outcomes for implementation research: Conceptual distinctions, measurement challenges, and research agenda. *Administration and Policy in Mental Health and Mental Health Services Research*. Advance online publication. doi:10.1007/s10488-010-0319-7

Quinby, R. K., Hanson, K., Brooke-Weiss, B., Arthur, M. W., Hawkins, J. D., & Fagan, A. A. (2008). Installing the Communities That Care prevention system: Implementation progress and fidelity in a randomized controlled trial. *Journal of Community Psychology, 36*(3), 313–332. doi:10.1002/jcop.20194

Rapp, C. A., Etzel-Wise, D., Marty, D., Coffman, M., Carlson, L., Asher, D., . . . & Holter M. (2009). Barriers to evidence-based practice implementation: Results of a qualitative study. *Community Mental Health Journal, 46*(2), 112–118. doi:10.1007/s10597-009-9238-z

Raudenbush, S. W., & Bryk, A. S. (2002). *Hierarchical linear models: Applications and data analysis methods.* Thousand Oaks, CA: Sage.

Real, K., & Poole, M. S. (2005). Innovation implementation: Conceptualization and measurement in organizational research. In R. W. Woodman, W. A. Pasmore, & A. B. Shani (Eds.), *Research in organizational change and development* (Vol. 15, pp. 63–134). Oxford, England: Elsevier.

Reid, P. T., & Vianna, E. (2001). Negotiating partnerships in research on poverty with community-based agencies. *Journal of Social Issues, 57*(2), 337–354. doi:10.1111/0022-4537.00217

Reynolds, A. J., & Temple, J. A. (1995). Quasi-experimental estimates of the effects of a preschool intervention: Psychometric and econometric comparisons. *Evaluation Review*, *19*(4), 347–373. doi:10.1177/0193841X9501900401

Robins, C. S., Ware, N. C., DosReis, S., Willging, C. E., Chung, J. Y., & Lewis-Fernández, R. (2008). Dialogues on mixed-methods and mental health services research: Anticipating challenges, building solutions. *Psychiatric Services*, *59*(7), 727–731. doi:10.1176/appi. ps.59.7.727

Robbins, S. P., Chatterjee, P., & Canda, E. R. (2006). *Contemporary human behavior theory: A critical perspective for social work* (2nd ed.). Boston, MA: Allyn and Bacon.

Rogers, E. M. (2003). *Diffusion of innovations* (5th ed.). New York, NY: Free Press.

Rogosa, D., Brandt, D., & Zimowski, M. (1982). A growth curve approach to the measurement of change. *Psychological Bulletin*, *92*(3), 726–748. doi:10.1037/0033-2909.92.3.726

Rosenbaum, P. R., & Rubin, D. B. (1984). Reducing bias in observational studies using subclassification on the propensity score. *Journal of the American Statistical Association*, *79*(387), 516–524.

Rosenheck, R. A. (2001). Organizational process: A missing link between research and practice. *Psychiatric Services*, *52*(12), 1607–1612.

Rousseau, D. (1990). Assessing organizational culture: The case for multiple methods. In B. Schneider (Ed.), *Organizational climate and culture* (pp. 153–192). San Francisco, CA: Jossey-Bass.

Rubin, A., & Babbie, E. R. (2008). *Research methods for social work* (6th ed.). Belmont, CA: Thomson Brooks/Cole.

Sackett, D. L., Richardson, W. S., Rosenberg, W., & Haynes, R. B. (1997). *Evidence-based medicine: How to practice and teach EBM*. New York, NY: Churchill Livingstone.

Sajatovic, M., Davies, M., Bauer, M. S., McBride, L., Hays, R. W., Safavi, R., & Jenkins, J. (2005). Attitudes regarding the collaborative practice model and treatment adherence among individuals with bipolar disorder. *Comprehensive Psychiatry*, *46*(4), 272–277. doi:10.1016/j.comppsych.2004.10.007

Sandelowski, M. (2000). Combining qualitative and quantitative sampling, data collection, and analysis techniques in mixed-method studies. *Research in Nursing & Health*, *23*(3), 246–255. doi:10.1002/1098-240X(200006)23:3<246::AID-NUR9>3.0.CO;2-H

Schoenwald, S. K. (2009). The transport and diffusion of Multisystemic Therapy. In R. K. McHugh & D. H. Barlow (Eds.), *The dissemination of evidence-based psychological treatments.* New York, NY: Oxford University Press.

Schoenwald, S. K. (2010). From policy pinball to purposeful partner-ship. The policy contexts of Multisystemic Therapy transport and dissemination. In J. R. Weisz & A. E. Kazdin (Eds.), *Evidence-based psychotherapies for children and adolescents* (pp. 538–553). New York, NY: Guilford Press.

Schoenwald, S. K., & Henggeler, S. W. (2004). A public health pers-pective on the transport of evidence-based practices. *Clinical Psycho-logy: Science and Practice, 11*(4), 360–363. doi:10.1093/clipsy.bph092

Schoenwald, S. K., Kelleher, K., Weisz, J. R., & the Research Network on Youth Mental Health. (2008). Building bridges to evidence-based practice: The MacArthur Foundation Child System and Treatment Enhancement Projects (Child STEPs). *Administration and Policy in Mental Health and Mental Health Services Research, 35*(1–2), 66–72. doi:10.1007/s10488-007-0160-9

Schoenwald, S. K., Sheidow, A. J., Letourneau, E. J., & Liao, J. G. (2003). Transportability of Multisystemic Therapy: Evidence for multi-level influences. *Mental Health Services Research, 5*(4), 223–239. doi:10.1023/A:1026229102151

Scrimshaw, S. C. M., & Hurtado, E. (1987). *Rapid assessment procedures for nutrition and primary health care: Anthropological approaches to improving programme effectiveness.* Los Angeles, CA: UCLA Latin American Center.

Sells, S. B., & James, L. R. (1988). Organizational climate. In J. R. Nesselroade & R. B. Cattell (Eds.), *Handbook of multivariate experimental psychology: Perspectives on Individual differences* (2nd ed., pp. 915–937). New York, NY: Plenum Press.

Shadish, W. R., Cook, T. D., & Campbell, D. T. (2002). *Experimental and quasi-experimental designs for generalized causal inference.* Boston, MA: Houghton Mifflin.

Shadish, W. R., & Ragsdale, K. (1996). Random versus nonrandom assignment in controlled experiments: Do you get the same answer? *Journal of Consulting and Clinical Psychology, 64*(6), 1290–1305. doi:10.1037/0022-006X.64.6.1290

Sheidow, A. J., Schoenwald, S. K., Wagner, H. R., Allred, C. A., & Burns, B. J. (2007). Predictors of workforce turnover in a transported treatment program. *Administration and Policy in Mental Health and Mental Health Services Research, 34*(1), 45–56. doi:10.1007/s10488-006-0061-3

Shortell, S. M., Zazzali, J. L., Burns, L. R., Alexander, J. A., Gillies, R. R., Budetti, P. P., . . . & Zuckerman, H. S. (2001). Implementing evidence-based medicine: the role of market pressures, compensation incentives, and culture in physician organizations. *Medical Care, 39*(7, Suppl. I), I62–I78.

Simpson, D. D. (2002). A conceptual framework for transferring research to practice. *Journal of Substance Abuse Treatment, 22*(4), 171–182. doi:10.1016/S0740–5472(02)00231–3

Slade, M., Gask, L., Leese, M., McCrone, P., Montana, C., Powell, R., . . . Chew-Graham, C. (2008). Failure to improve appropriateness of referrals to adult community mental health services—lessons from a multi-site cluster randomized controlled trial. *Family Practice, 25*(3), 181–190. doi:10.1093/fampra/cmn025

Social Development Research Group. (2005). *Community Youth Development Study, Youth Development Survey [Grades 5–7].* Seattle, WA: Social Development Research Group, School of Social Work, University of Washington.

Social Work Policy Institute. (2010). *Comparative effectiveness research and social work: Strengthening the connection.* Retrieved from http://www.socialworkpolicy.org/wp-content/uploads/2010/03/SWPI-CER-Full-RPT-FINAL.pdf

Sofaer, S. (1999). Qualitative methods: What are they and why use them? *Health Services Research, 34*(5, part 2), 1101–1118.

Sosna, T., & Marsenich, L. (2006). *Community Development Team model: Supporting the model adherent implementation of programs and practices.* Sacramento, CA: California Institute of Mental Health. Retrieved from http://www.cimh.org/downloads/CDT_report.pdf

Soydan, H. (2008). Applying randomized controlled trials and systematic reviews in social work research. *Research on Social Work Practice, 18*(4), 311–318. doi:10.1177/1049731507307788

Soydan, H. (Guest Ed.). (2009). Implementation and translational research [Special issue]. *Research on Social Work Practice, 19*(5).

Soydan, H., Mullen, E. J., Alexandra, L., Rehnman, J., & Li, Y.-P. (2010). Evidence-based clearinghouses in social work. *Research on Social Work Practice, 20*(6), 690–700. doi:10.1177/1049731510367436

Sperber, E., McKay, M. M., Bell, C. C., Petersen, I., Bhana, A., & Paikoff, R. (2008). Adapting and disseminating a community-collaborative, evidence-based HIV/AIDS prevention programme: Lessons from the history of CHAMP. *Vulnerable Children and Youth Studies, 3*(2), 150–158. doi:10.1080/17450120701867561

Steckler, A., McLeroy, K. R., Goodman, R. M., Bird, S. T., & McCormick, L. (1992). Toward integrating qualitative and quantitative methods: An introduction. *Health Education & Behavior, 19*(1), 1–8. doi:10.1177/109019819201900101

Stern, S. B., Alaggia, R., Watson, K., & Morton, T. R. (2008). Implementing an evidence-based parenting program with adherence in the real world of community practice. *Research on Social Work Practice, 18*(6), 543–554. doi:10.1177/1049731507308999

Strand, K., Marullo, S., Cutforth, N., Stoecker, R., & Donohue, P. (2003). *Community-based research and higher education: Principles and practices.* San Francisco, CA: Jossey-Bass.

Strauss, A. L., & Corbin, J. M. (1998). *Basics of qualitative research: Techniques and procedures for developing grounded theory* (2nd ed.). Thousand Oaks, CA: Sage.

Sundell, K., Hansson, K., Löfholm, C. A., Olsson, T., Gustle, L.-H., & Kadesjö, C. (2008). The transportability of Multisystemic Therapy to Sweden: Short-term results from a randomized trial of conduct-disordered youth. *Journal of Family Psychology, 22*(4), 550–560. doi:10.1037/a0012790

Tashakkori, A., & Teddlie, C. (1998). *Mixed methodology: Combining the qualitative and quantitative approaches.* Thousand Oaks, CA: Sage.

Tashakkori, A., & Teddlie, C. (Eds.). (2003). *Handbook of mixed methods in social and behavioral research.* Thousand Oaks, CA: Sage.

Teddlie, C., & Tashakkori, A. (2003). Major issues and controversies in the use of mixed methods in the social and behavioral sciences. In A. Tashakkori & C. Teddlie (Eds.), *Handbook of mixed methods in the social and behavioral sciences* (pp. 3–50). Thousand Oaks, CA: Sage.

Ten Have, T. R., Coyne, J., Salzer, M., & Katz, I. (2003). Research to improve the quality of care for depression: Alternatives to the simple randomized clinical trial. *General Hospital Psychiatry, 25*(2), 115–123. doi:10.1016/S0163-8343(02)00275-X

Ten Have, T. R., Joffe, M., & Cary, M. (2003). Causal logistic models for non-compliance under randomized treatment with univariate binary response. *Statistics in Medicine, 22*(8), 1255–1283. doi:10.1002/sim.1401

Tervalon, M., & Murray-Garcia, J. (1998). Cultural humility versus cultural competence: A critical distinction in defining physician training outcomes in multicultural education. *Journal of Health Care for the Poor and Underserved, 9*(2), 117–125.

Thomas, S. B., & Quinn, S. C. (1991). The Tuskegee Syphilis Study, 1932–1972: Implications for HIV education and AIDS risk education programs in the black community. *American Journal of Public Health, 81*(11), 1495–1505.

Trochim, W. M. (1989). An introduction to concept mapping for planning and evaluation. *Evaluation and Program Planning, 12*(1), 1–16. doi:10.1016/0149-7189(89)90016-5

U.S. Department of Health and Human Services. (1999). *Mental health: A report of the surgeon general.* Rockville, MD: Substance Abuse and Mental Health Services Administration & National Institutes of Health. Retrieved from http://www.surgeongeneral.gov/library/mentalhealth/home.html

Valente, T. W. (1995). *Network models of the diffusion of innovations.* Creskill, NJ: Hampton Press.

Valente, T. W. (2010). *Social networks and health: Models, methods, and applications.* New York, NY: Oxford University Press.

Vangen, S., & Huxham, C. (2003). Nurturing collaborative relations: Building trust in interorganizational collaboration. *Journal of Applied Behavioral Science, 39*(1), 5–31. doi:10.1177/0021886303039001001

Viswanathan, M., Ammerman, A., Eng, E., Gartlehner, G., Lohr, K. N., Griffith, D., . . . & Whitener, L. (2004). *Community-based participatory research: Assessing the evidence* (AHRQ Publication No. 04-E022-2). Rockville, MD: Agency for Health Care Research and Quality. Retrieved from http://www.ahrq.gov/downloads/pub/evidence/pdf/cbpr/cbpr.pdf

Wallerstein, N. B., & Duran, B. (2006). Using community-based participatory research to address health disparities. *Health Promotion Practice, 7*(3), 312–323. doi:10.1177/1524839906289376

Wandersman, A., Duffy, J., Flaspohler, P., Noonan, R., Lubell, K., Stillman, L., . . . Saul, J. (2008). Bridging the gap between prevention research and practice: The Interactive Systems Framework for Dissemination and Implementation. *American Journal of Community Psychology, 41*(3–4), 171–181. doi:10.1007/s10464-008-9174-z

Ware, J. E., Jr., Kosinski, M., & Keller, S. D. (1996). A 12-item short-form health survey: Construction of scales and preliminary tests of reliability and validity. *Medical Care, 34*(3), 220–223.

Waszak, C., & Sines, M. C. (2003). Mixed methods in psychological research. In A. Tashakkori & C. Teddlie (Eds.), *Handbook of mixed methods in the social and behavioral sciences* (pp. 557–576). Thousand Oaks, CA: Sage.

Webster-Stratton, C., Reid, M. J., & Stoolmiller, M. (2008). Preventing conduct problems and improving school readiness: Evaluation of the Incredible Years teacher and child training programs in high-risk schools. *Journal of Child Psychology and Psychiatry, 49*(5), 471–488. doi:10.1111/j.1469-7610.2007.01861.x

Weisz, J. R., Chorpita, B. F., Frye, A., Ng, M. Y., Lau, N., Bearman, S. K., . . . & the Research Network on Youth Mental Health. (2011). Youth top problems: Using idiographic, consumer-guided assessment to identify treatment needs and to track change during psychotherapy. *Journal of Consulting and Clinical Psychology, 79*(3), 369–380. doi:10.1037/a0023307

Weisz, J. R., Thurber, C. A., Sweeney, L., Proffitt, V. D., & LeGagnoux, G. L. (1997). Brief treatment of mild-to-moderate child depression using primary and secondary control enhancement training. *Journal of Consulting and Clinical Psychology, 65*(4), 703–707. doi:10.1037/0022-006X.65.4.703

Weller, E. B., Weller, R. A., Rooney, M. T., & Fristad, M. A. (1999a). *ChIPS: Children's Interview for Psychiatric Syndromes.* Washington, DC: American Psychiatric Publishing.

Weller, E. B., Weller, R. A., Rooney, M. T., & Fristad, M. A. (1999b). *P-ChIPS: Children's Interview for Psychiatric Syndromes–Parent Version.* Washington, DC: American Psychiatric Publishing.

Wells, K. B., Miranda, J., Bruce, M. L., Alegria, M., & Wallerstein, N. (2004). Bridging community intervention and mental health services research. *American Journal of Psychiatry, 161*(6), 955–963.

Wells, K. B., Sherbourne, C., Schoenbaum, M., Duan, N., Meredith, L., Unützer, J., . . . & Rubenstein, L. V. (2000). Impact of disseminating quality improvement programs for depression in managed primary care: A randomized controlled trial. *Journal of the American Medical Association, 283*(2), 212–220. doi:10.1001/jama.283.2.212

Wells, K. B, Staunton, A., Norris, K. C., & the CHIC Council. (2006). Building an academic-community partnered network for clinical services research: The Community Health Improvement Collaborative (CHIC). *Ethnicity and Disease, 16*(1, Suppl. 1), S3–S17.

West, S. G., Duan, N., Pequegnat, W., Gaist, P., Des Jarlais, D. C., Holtgrave, D., . . . & Mullen, P. D. (2008). Alternatives to the randomized controlled trial. *American Journal of Public Health, 98*(8), 1359–1366. doi:10.2105/AJPH.2007.124446

Westfall, J. M., Mold. J., & Fagnan, L. (2007). Practice-based research—"Blue highways" on the NIH Roadmap. *Journal of American Medical Association, 297*(4), 403–406. doi:10.1001/jama.297.4.403

Wethington, E., Breckman, R., Meador, R., Reid, M. C., Sabir, M., Lachs, M., & Pillemer, K. A. (2007). The CITRA pilot studies program: Mentoring translational research. *Gerontologist, 47*(6), 845–850. doi:10.1093/geront/47.6.845

Willms, D. G., Best, J. A., Taylor, D. W., Gilbert, J. R., Wilson, D. M. C., Lindsay, E. A., & Singer, J. (1990). A systematic approach for using qualitative methods in primary prevention research. *Medical Anthropology Quarterly, 4*(4), 391–409. doi:10.1525/maq.1990. 4.4.02a00020

Wittkampf, K. A., Naeije, L., Schene, A. H., Huyser, J., & Van Weert, H. C. (2007). Diagnostic accuracy of the mood module of the Patient Health Questionnaire: A systematic review. *General Hospital Psychiatry, 29*(5), 388–395. doi:10.1016/j.genhosppsych. 2007.06.004

Woltmann, E. M., Whitley, R., McHugo, G. J., Brunette, M., Torrey, W. C., Coots, L., . . . & Drake, R. E. (2008). The role of staff turnover in the implementation of evidence-based practices in mental health care. *Psychiatric Services, 59*(7), 732–737. doi:10.1176/appi. ps.59.7.732

Wong, M. (2006). Commentary: Building partnerships between schools and academic partners to achieve a health-related research agenda. *Ethnicity and Disease, 16*(1, Suppl. 1), S149–S153.

Wright, C. C., & Sim, J. (2003). Intention-to-treat approach to data from randomized controlled trials: A sensitivity analysis. *Journal of Clinical Epidemiology, 56*(9), 833–842.

Zazzali, J. L., Sherbourne, C., Hoagwood, K. E., Greene, D., Bigley, M. F., & Sexton, T. L. (2008). The adoption and implementation of an evidence based practice in child and family mental health services organizations: A pilot study of Functional Family Therapy in New York State. *Administration and Policy in Mental Health and Mental Health Services Research, 35*(1–2), 38–49. doi:10.1007/s10488-007-0145-8

Zerhouni, E. (2003). The NIH Roadmap. *Science, 302*(5642), 63–72. doi:10.1126/science.1091867

Ziman, J. (2000). *Real science: What it is and what it means.* Cambridge, England: Cambridge University Press.

Index

CPSIA information can be obtained at www.ICGtesting.com
Printed in the USA
BVOW070717071111

275445BV00003B/4/P

9 780195 398489